Searchlights for S
Year 2 Teacher's Book

Chris Buckton   Pie Corbett

Contents

Introduction		iii
Scope and Sequence Chart		vii
Term 1 Unit 1	'Long' vowel phonemes and **ow**	2
Unit 2	'Long' and 'short' **oo**	4
Unit 3	Plural **s**	6
Unit 4	Adding **ed**	8
Unit 5	Adding **ing**	10
Unit 6	Vowel phonemes **ar** and **oy**	12
Term 2 Unit 7	Vowel phoneme **air**	14
Unit 8	Syllables	16
Unit 9	Vowel phoneme **er**	18
Unit 10	Vowel phoneme **or**	20
Unit 11	Digraphs **wh ch ph** and **f** phoneme	22
Unit 12	Negative prefixes and opposites	24
Term 3 Unit 13	Same spelling pattern, different sounds	26
Unit 14	Vowel phoneme **ear**	28
Unit 15	Adding suffix **ly (ful)**	30
Unit 16	**ea** and **ear**	32
Unit 17	Revising vowel phonemes	34
Unit 18	Revision – phonemic spelling, syllables	36
Additional Unit 1	Compound words	38
Additional Unit 2	Revision of prefixes and suffixes; puzzle letter	40
Additional Unit 3	Synonyms	42
Facsimile Big Book pages		46

CAMBRIDGE UNIVERSITY PRESS

Searchlights for Spelling

Searchlights for Spelling is a comprehensive spelling scheme for Years 2–6/Primary 3–7 that covers all the word-level spelling objectives of the National Literacy Strategy (NLS) and meets the requirements of the National Curriculum.

It is a systematic scheme for teaching the patterns of the English spelling system through stimulating, multi-sensory activities. It builds up spelling concepts through an investigative approach, equipping children with the skills to tackle new words as well as developing their strategies for the recall of key words and spelling patterns.

The scheme also builds on NLS programmes such as Progression in Phonics (PiPs) and Spelling Bank and is cross-referenced to them, making use of their basic interactive techniques such as 'Get Up and Go', 'Show Me', and 'Time Out' (see Key terms overleaf for further explanation).

Spelling for writing

The reason for learning to spell is to become fluent in everyday writing. *Searchlights* is designed to equip children to write fluently, rather than simply to learn and be tested upon decontextualised lists of words. It aims to make spelling enjoyable, through developing a sense of curiosity about words and an awareness of language patterns.

The sessions begin by deepening children's *understanding* of an objective or strategy, through direct teaching or investigation. This is followed by *applying* their understanding through shared writing and independent activities. It is important to ensure that spelling objectives are always emphasised in the children's own writing, in order to reinforce the concept of spelling for a purpose.

A multi-sensory approach

The activities are based on four key learning styles:

- visual – remembering common patterns; writing words down to check whether they 'look' right; looking at the 'tricky' bit and trying the letters in a different order; looking for words within words; seeing the word in your mind, holding a word in your memory by seeing it, then looking to the top left of your mind to recall.
- aural and oral – hearing and pronouncing words; emphasising or exaggerating pronunciation to aid learning (e.g. *Wed-nes-day*); breaking words into syllables or phonemes; remembering some words with a rhythmic strategy (e.g. *Mrs d*, *Mrs i*, *Mr ffi*, *Mr c*, *Mr u*, *Mrs lty*: *difficulty*); using rhyme to spell by analogy.
- kinaesthetic – writing common patterns; tracing over words; sky-writing as you say each letter; getting the feel of common handwriting joins.
- cognitive – knowing rules, conventions, possible and impossible combinations; identifying word roots, suffixes and prefixes; using knowledge of grammar (e.g. *ed* – past tense), using mnemonics (e.g. *there is a rat in separate*).

By experiencing a multi-sensory teaching approach, children who learn in different ways have every chance of developing their ability to spell. Good spellers use a range of strategies. The whole class and pupil activities in the scheme use a variety of approaches. To further support multi-sensory teaching, the above symbols are given next to the quickfire activities for each unit – Oddbods and Snip-snaps (see Key terms, page vi).

Identifying and representing phonemes

Searchlights generally follows the NLS Framework conventions for identifying and representing phonemes, including the use of 'long' and 'short' to distinguish certain vowel phonemes. For the most part *Searchlights* adopts other NLS terminology. Phonemes are represented by bold type in all materials, while letter patterns are red in the Teacher's Book, Big Book and Pupil's Book and underlined in the Photocopy Masters Book.

It is important to note that the teaching of certain phonemes and their associated letter patterns can be affected by regional variation in pronunciation. You will need to adapt your teaching of these phonemes to suit the needs of your class. Such instances are noted in the relevant units.

Spelling practice – little and often

Children need frequent practice so that spelling becomes automatic and does not interfere with the act of composition. *Searchlights* is designed to be

Searchlights for Spelling

as flexible as possible and can be used in a variety of ways, depending on the needs of the children. The activities fit naturally into word-level work within the literacy hour and have a simple, regular pattern. They can be adapted for different classes and groups.

Spelling and handwriting

Searchlights emphasises the important link between spelling and handwriting, particularly in Year 2. Regular practice of handwriting joins helps to consolidate the learning of common letter strings. A joined script is offered wherever it is intended that a child will copy or continue writing.

Spelling log

It is helpful for children to develop the habit of keeping a personal spelling log. It can contain:

- collections of words arising from the independent activities;
- lists of oddbods (see Key terms below) and other 'tricky' words;
- results of spelling investigations;
- dictations and other tests;
- personal spelling targets;
- useful strategies or mnemonics;
- space for **Look Say Cover Write Check** practice.

A possible format for a spelling log is included in the Photocopy Masters Book for those who want to make use of it. Reference pages in the Pupil's Book, and extra pages in the Big Book, also provide useful material which the children could transfer to their log.

How to use *Searchlights for Spelling*

Key terms

Brush-ups:	activities which revisit objectives from the previous year, for those children who need more time to catch up.
Catch-you-out:	a word that is an exception to a specific rule or teaching point (e.g. where a word changes completely when forming a plural rather than just adding s or es).
Get Up and Go:	individual children come out to the front to demonstrate something.
Oddbod:	a 'tricky' word that causes common difficulties (featured on the Big Book left hand page and in the list of words to learn in each unit).
Time Out / Show Me:	all children can respond by writing on dry-wipe boards and showing the spelling attempt.
Sky-writing:	drawing the shape of a letter or word in the air as an aid to memory.
Snip-snaps:	short, snappy ideas for further practice in applying the unit's objective or in learning key words.
Spelling log:	a personal ongoing record of words being learnt (see Photocopy Masters Book page 3).
Think about…/ Extra challenge:	both these suggestions take the children a little further in exploring or applying a spelling concept.

A glossary is provided on page 44.

Colour-coding

Red type is used to highlight target letters and letter patterns. To highlight phonemes and distinguish them from spelling patterns, they are printed in bold type.

(In the Photocopy Masters Book, where colour is not used, letters and letter patterns are underlined and phonemes are in bold.)

The components

For each year there are four key components:

- **Teacher's Book** – containing a double-page spread of step-by-step notes for each unit's teaching as well as background information and a glossary.
- **Big Book** (or OHTs for Years 5–6/Primary 6–7) – containing a double-page spread of whole-class material for each unit as well as useful revision and supporting material.
- **Pupil's Book** – containing a double-page spread of differentiated activities for each unit and reference pages with word lists and reminders of spelling rules and strategies.
- **Photocopy Masters Book** – containing a photocopiable homework copymaster (PCM) for each unit as well as revision activities, assessment material and guidance for parents.

Together these resources provide 18 core units of work for the year (six units a term). Three additional units provide further material, which can be fitted in as necessary. Each unit comprises two parts:

- Part 1 – introduces the spelling objective(s).
- Part 2 – takes the objective(s) one step further, or introduces a further objective, and provides a test dictation.

Part 1

Teaching the objective(s): Swift, lively interactive teaching of objective(s), using the left hand page of the Big Book. Plus teaching of key words, including 'oddbods' (see Key terms).

Using the objective(s): Developing the skill or concept through writing, including brief opportunities for shared writing.

Independent work (Pupil's Book): Differentiated activities focusing on reinforcement and extension of target objectives (see Differentiation, following). This may take place as part of a literacy hour, or at another time.

Review (plenary): Review of independent work and recap of main teaching points.

Homework: Reinforcement task generally with an investigative element which can involve other family members; Words to Learn for the unit's dictation.

Part 2

An extended whole class session.

Teaching the objective(s): Usually revisiting and developing the unit focus, using the right-hand page of the Big Book.

Using the objective(s): Writing with the class, pausing and discussing spelling points.

Review (plenary): Review and summary of new learning, and discussion of homework findings.

Follow-up homework: This allows for further exploration or reinforcement of learning.

Test dictation: Class dictation that includes examples of the spelling objective and oddbod(s) for the week.

Differentiation

Independent activities in the Pupil's Book are differentiated at three levels, A, B and C. A and B activities consolidate children's learning of the key objectives of the unit, while C activities are more challenging or address a further objective. C activities may anticipate Part 2. Children could work through all three when appropriate. The Extra challenge in some units extends children's learning further.

Children who find spelling particularly difficult may need extra time to revisit key objectives from the previous year or years. For Year 2/Primary 3 children who need extra phonics teaching, use activities for the earlier steps in the NLS Progression in Phonics (PiPs). *Searchlights* also provides a bank of Brush-up ideas based on the previous year's objectives as well as six extra revision PCMs.

For each unit, the Words to Learn list on the homework PCM is differentiated (A, B, C) so that some children can be given fewer target words to learn.

Paired spelling

Children could spend ten minutes every day following this simple procedure in order to learn their individual lists (between five and ten words at a time). This procedure could also be introduced to parents and it is given as part of the 'How to help your child with spelling' guidance (see the Photocopy Masters Book, pages 47–48).

Searchlights for Spelling

- The child reads the word; says it aloud; spells the letters out; tries to spell it out without looking.
- Together, parent/partner and child discuss 'tricky bits' and devise a way of remembering them.
- If the child finds the word hard to remember, repeat the first two stages as necessary before attempting to write.
- The spelling partner/parent covers the word.
- The child writes it down.
- Together they check – if incorrect, revisit two or three more times.

Assessment

The units include a dictation test as well as a termly SATs-style test to track progress. To be useful, spelling tests should always be diagnostic. Look carefully at the results to find out what strategies the children are using. It is important, too, not to penalise them for incorrect but intelligent, plausible guesses. One useful approach is to allocate two marks to each word: the first mark could be given if the target phoneme, pattern or rule is correct (e.g. *ai* spelt correctly in *rain*) and the second if the whole word is correct.

A simple Tracking sheet to help you monitor children's progress is provided in the Photocopy Masters Book (pages 3–5). Children's involvement in assessing their own progress in spelling is very important. To encourage children to review their own learning, yearly self-assessment sheets with 'I can' targets are also provided (see Photocopy Masters Book, page 4).

Test dictation

The object of regular dictation is to give the children practice in spelling words in context, reinforcing the importance of accurate spelling in writing.

Searchlights dictation provides three levels of differentiated sentences for each unit. The children learn the words before they are tested on some of them in context. In Year 2/Primary 3 there are ten words to learn per unit: comprising words related to the unit's objective(s); and wherever possible words are drawn from the NLS list of high frequency words; the oddbod(s).

Test scores and comments can be recorded on the teacher Tracking sheet (see Photocopy Masters Book pages 3–5). The suggested procedure for the test dictation is as follows.

Introduction (first unit)

- Explain to the children what a dictation is.
- Tell them that you will be dictating sentences.

Procedure

- Tell them that first, you'll read the whole sentence while they listen. Specify whether you want them to write out the whole sentence or just the target word.
- Then explain that you'll read a little bit at a time while they write it down (if they are writing out the whole sentence).
- Tell them what to do if they come to a word they don't know: try to break the word up into its sounds, or think of another rhyming word which perhaps they can remember how to spell.
- Give prompts where appropriate, e.g. reminding them of rules or asking questions such as: *Remember that oddbod? Listen to that word again – what sound can you hear?*
- Read the passage through again so that they can check their writing.
- Note: Make sure that you do not expose strugglers. Children should simply write the words they have learnt (A, A/B, A/B/C). There is no need to draw attention to difference here.

Homework

For each unit, a homework PCM provides the related list of words to learn for the dictation test and a task that reinforces the unit's teaching, or focuses on revision. The sheets also encourage an investigative approach. Words to Learn for each unit are offered in three levels of difficulty. They are referred to as key words in the Photocopy Masters Book and listed there in full on page 6.

Parents/carers are offered further guidance on a separate PCM: 'How to help your child with spelling'.

Scope and sequence chart – Year 2

Unit	NLS Objectives	Big Book	Pupil's Book	Homework PCM	Snip-snaps	Oddbods
1 'Long' vowel phonemes and **ow**	NLS 2.1.W1, W2, W3, W4, W12	**ow/ou** Name rhymes	Spelling **ow, i-e, ee, oo**	Mainly **ai** ('long' vowel investigation)	Word Sort Word Families Odd One Out	again
2 'Long' and 'short' **oo**	NLS 2.1.W2, W3, W4, W5, W9, W12	Long or short **oo**? Using **oo**	Hearing 'long' and 'short' **oo**	Key word thief	Phoneme Frame Word Chain Remember these Words	could, should, would
3 Plural **s**	NLS 2.1.W2, W4, W7, W9, W12	Noah's Ark Old Macdonald's Farm	Adding plural **s**	Animal alphabet	Plain Jane Quickfire Catch-you-outs Noun Clues	to, too, two
4 Adding **ed**	NLS 2.1.W2, W5, W7, W9, W12	Hearing **t, d, id** endings Nat's holiday	Add **ed**; the different sounds of **ed**	Catch-you-outs	Letter Fans Rhyming Families Spelling Soccer	people
5 Adding **ing**	NLS 2.1.W7, W8, W9, W10, W12	The Cataract at Lodore **ing** or **ed**?	Adding **ing**	Key word sort	Key Word Tower Word Sort Word Shapes	said
6 Vowel phonemes **ar** and **oy**	NLS 2.1.W2, W3, W5, W9, W12	**ar** **oy**	Making **ar** words	Oddbod round-up	**ie** investigation Full Circle Word Caterpillar	laugh
7 Vowel phoneme **air**	NLS 2.2.W1, W2, W6, W9, W14	Beware the bear! Milly and Billy went to the Fair	Sorting **air** words	Beware the bear!	Homophones Odd One Out Quiz Kim's Game	there, where
8 Syllables	NLS 2.2.W5, W6, W9, W10, W14	Syllable School Register Syllable poems	Counting syllables	Little Arabella Miller	Spelling Long Words Can't Catch Me Sandwich Fillings	another
9 Vowel phoneme **er**	NLS 2.2.W2, W6, W9, W13, W14	Sorting **er** words People who …	Making silly **er** sentences	Crossword	Spelling Race Magnetic Multiplication Key Word Sentence Race	were
10 Vowel phoneme **or**	NLS 2.2.W2, W6, W9, W13, W14	**or** Animal sports report	Making silly **or** sentences	More about **or**	Phoneme Frame Full Circle Key Word Battle	door
11 Digraphs **wh ch** and **f** phoneme	NLS 2.2.W3, W6, W9, W13, W14	**wh, ch, ph** Sorting **f** words	Finding **wh** words; writing questions with **wh**	Consonant pairs with **h**	Question Time Name Sounds Inflectional Endings	who
12 Negative prefixes and opposites	NLS 2.2.W6, W8, W9, W14	Using prefixes Opposites	Adding prefixes **un, mis** and **dis**	Oddbod round-up	Prefix Family Opposites Key Word Hunt	once

Scope and sequence chart – Year 2 cont.

Unit	NLS Objectives	Big Book	Pupil's Book	Homework PCM	Snip-snaps	Oddbods
13 Same spelling pattern, different sounds	NLS 2.3.W6, W8, W9, W12	Finding the odd one out Tongue twisters	Finding rhymes for o, our and one	All ears!	Phoneme Snap Guess the Subject Split Digraphs	some, come
14 Vowel phoneme ear	NLS 2.3.W1, W3, W4, W8, W11, W12	Sorting ear words Rhymes	Sorting words with the ear sound and with the ear letter pattern	15 minute challenge!	Hear ear Rhyme Ball Jumbly	here, hear
15 Adding suffixes ly (ful)	NLS 2.3.W6, W7, W8, W11, W12	Adding ly Nicely, nicely	Adding suffix ly	Be careful!	Opposite Meanings The Adverb Game Key Word Clues	because
16 ea and ear	NLS 2.3.W1, W3, W6, W11, W12	ea words Long and short e	Discriminating between 'long' and 'short' ea	Word endings	Head, Ear or Seat? Postbox Full Circle	after
17 Revising vowel phonemes	NLS 2.1.W3, 2.2.W2, 2.3.W1, W4, W8, W11, W12	Wordsearch 'Long' vowel limericks	Solving a wordsearch with 'long' vowel words	Wordsearch	Phoneme Chain Which Looks Right? Living Sentences	first
18 Revision – phonemic spelling, syllables	NLS 2.3.W1, W2, W4, W8, W11, W12	Hidden words Vowel sounds, split digraphs	Finding hidden words in reading books	Oddbod round-up	Word Factory Word Frames Ladder Game	want
Additional 1 Compound words	NLS 2.2.W4, W6, W9, W14	Compound words Working out the meaning of compound words	Making compound words	Compound words for the word wall	Word Wall Compound Clues Shannon's Game	their
Additional 2 Revision of prefixes and suffixes; puzzle letter	NLS 2.2.W8, 2.3.W7, W8, W11, W12	Prefixes and suffixes Puzzle letter	Adding prefixes and suffixes	Suffix hunt	Quick Change Key Word Tennis Clusters Competition	eight
Additional 3 Synonyms	NLS 2.2.W11, 2.3.W10, W12	Synonyms for 'big' and 'small' Synonym nursery rhymes	Finding synonyms	A BIG challenge	Synonym Pelmanism Antonyms Word Hunt	many

1 'Long' vowel phonemes and ow

Objectives for Unit 1
Revision of **ai**, **ee**, **ie**, **oa**, **oo**; introducing **ow**

Part 1

You need Big Book page 2; dry-wipe boards or notebooks; Pupil's Book pages 2–3; PCM 1

Whole class
- Introduce the objective: different ways of spelling the same phoneme.
- Tune in by recapping simple spellings for **ee**, *e.g.* s*ea*, b*ee*, m*e*.
- Focus on the BBk page. Look at the pictures.
- Ask the children to say the words, then ask what sound is repeated (**ow**). Say it together.
- Ask them to find two ways to spell the phoneme **ow**.
- Time Out/Show Me: ask the children to try out spellings on dry-wipe boards.
- Get Up and Go: choose children to write words on the BBk page.
- Look for patterns, e.g. *house/mouse*.
- Make up sentences for **ow** phoneme. Write them on the board, demonstrating horizontal joins for handwriting. Use a second colour to show, e.g. ow and ou
    *I f*ou*nd a m*ou*se ar*ou*nd the h*ou*se.*
    *H*ow *n*ow *br*ow*n c*ow*?*
    *Sh*out *o*ut *d*ow*n the sp*out *and r*ou*nd the t*ow*n.*
- Show Me / Get Up and Go: children make up new sentences to contribute.
- Introduce the oddbod: *again* – see below.

Pupil activities
A and B: Read sentences and sort words into lists with different spellings for the same phoneme.
 A: ow and ou
 B: i-e, ie, y, igh
 C: Read sentences and list words with **ee** and **oo** phonemes, adding more words of their own.

Extra challenge: Think of other spelling patterns for the phonemes **ee** and **oo** (m**oo**n).

Review
Ask groups B and C to tell the class some ways of spelling phonemes **ie**, **ee** and **oo**. Make lists of spellings on large sheets for future reference.

Homework
ai investigation

Oddbod *again*
- Look for words within the word – *a*, *gain*.
- Link with other ai words, e.g. *will it r*ai*n ag*ai*n?*
- Practise writing the word swiftly.

Snip-snap Word Sort (see PiPs p. 34)
- Write *show* on a post-it. Remind children that sometimes the **ow** spelling is pronounced **oa**.
- Ask the children to call out rhyming words. Write them on post-its.
- Get Up and Go: children arrange the post-its in sets e.g. o, ow, oa, ough, o-e.

'Long' vowel phonemes and ow

NLS objectives for Unit 1				
2.1.W1	2.1.W2	2.1.W3	2.1.W4	2.1.W12

Part 2

You need Big Book page 3; dry-wipe boards or notebooks

Whole class
- Say together 'long' vowel phonemes **ai**, **ee**, **ie**, **oa**, **oo**.
- Recap: same phonemes can have different spellings.
- Look at the BBk page. Read the rhymes together.
- Ask children to provide rhymes for *Joe*, *June* and *Mike*, writing on dry-wipe boards.
- Brainstorm some more names with 'long' vowels. Focus on names with one syllable, so that the spelling of the 'long' vowels is clear, e.g. *Sue*, *Zane*, *Clive*.
- Make up more rhymes for the names, noticing spellings for each vowel phoneme.
- Use a different colour for the letter patterns and demonstrate horizontal joins for handwriting.

Review
- Ask the children:
  - How many ways can you spell the phoneme **ow**? (at least two ways: ow, ou)
  - **ai**? (at least three ways: ai, ay, a-e)
  - **oa**? (at least three ways: o, oa, o-e)
- Make lists of words for each spelling. Collect them on a large sheet for future reference. Children can also write them in their spelling logs/books.
- Homework review.
- Cover the following points:
  - a-e is the most common spelling.
  - ay very often comes at the end of words.
  - Make a list of the different spellings.

Follow-up homework
- Children write out examples of the different *ai* spellings using handwriting joins.

Test dictation
- OB We went home again.
- A The boy ran down the hill. We are at school now.
- B Bill has a red bike. People can't fly.
- C I had a bad dream.

Snip-snap Word Families
- Explain that if you know how to spell one word you can often work out how to spell others that are like it.
- Ask children to spell a key word, e.g. *play*, *tree*, *school*, *cat*, *look*, *and*. Write these up.
- Generate rhyming words which are spelt the same way.

Snip-snap Odd One Out
- Explain that you're going to read out a list of words and although they all rhyme one of them is spelt differently from the others, e.g.:
  - *he*, *she*, *we*, *see* (**ee**)
  - *low*, *no*, *so*, *go* (**oa**)
  - *came*, *aim*, *same*, *name* (**ai**)
- Children put hands up when they find the odd one out, and explain why. Some children may need to write the words down.

3

2 'Long' and 'short' oo

Objective for Unit 2

'Long' and 'short' **oo** phonemes ('long' **oo** = PiPs **ue**)

Part 1

You need Big Book page 4; dry-wipe boards or notebooks; Pupil's Book pages 4–5; PCM 2

Whole class
- N.B. The distribution of these sounds varies regionally (e.g. some dialects pronounce *room* with a 'short' **oo**, others with 'long' **oo**) – discuss as necessary.
- Introduce the objective: spelling the 'long' and 'short' **oo** phonemes (as in *pool* and *pull*).
- Look at the BBk page. Say the words with the children (*foot, hook, book, bull, stool*). Ask: which is the odd-one-out? (*stool*)
- Say the words *full, fool, good* and ask the children to spot the odd one out. (*fool*)
- Write these words on the board, commenting on the different ways of spelling the same phoneme and highlighting the letter patterns (e.g. underlining them).
- Time Out/Show Me: try out spellings of the BBk words on dry-wipe boards.
- Get Up and Go: choose children to write words on BBk page.
- Identify the different ways of spelling 'short' **oo**. (u, oo)
- Ask the children to provide rhymes for *stool, bull, book*. Look for patterns and exceptions, e.g. u before double l; ook words are usually 'short'; ool words are usually 'long' (though there are exceptions to these rules as well, e.g. *spook, wool*).
- Write up a short rhyme, using children's suggestions, e.g. *The fool sat on the stool.*
- Introduce the oddbods *could, should, would* ('short' **oo**) – see below.

Pupil activities
A: Spot the odd one out from three sets of words, distinguishing between **oo** sounds.
B: Sort 'long' and 'short' **oo** words in a story, then think of more words for each list.
C: Find rhyming words for 'long ' and 'short' **oo** words.

Extra challenge: Think of **oo** words to match letter patterns but with different sounds.

Review
- Ask children to recall the ways of spelling the 'short' **oo** phoneme. Remind them that the same spelling can make a different sound, e.g. *good* and *food*.

Homework
Children put the missing letters in key words.

Oddbods could, should, would
- Briefly discuss what the words mean.
- Ask a volunteer to ring the letters that spell the **oo** phoneme. (ou).
- Identify the first phonemes and underline their letters. (c, sh, w)
- Which letter can't you hear? (l)
- Do **Look Say Cover Write Check**.

Snip-snap Phoneme Frame
(see PiPs p. 22)
- Draw three boxes on the board. Say a word, e.g. *bush*.
- Ask children to identify the first phoneme and its letter b.
- Write the letter in the first box of the frame.
- Continue with the remaining two phonemes: the 'short' **oo** and **sh**.

'Long' and 'short' oo

NLS objectives for Unit 2					
2.1.W2	2.1.W3	2.1.W4	2.1.W5	2.1.W9	2.1.W12

Part 2

You need Big Book page 5; dry-wipe boards or notebooks

Whole class
- Look at the BBk page. Read the **oo** story together.
- Get Up and Go: ask children to circle the 'short' **oo** phonemes.
- Recap: same phonemes can have different spellings.
- Brainstorm some more 'short' **oo** words and compose a sentence, e.g. *He looked like a crook.*
- Time Out: ask the children to think of sentences using 'short' **oo** phonemes.
- Brainstorm a title for a 'long' **oo** story, e.g. *Cool Pool.*
- Ask children to contribute 'long' **oo** words and make a list on the board.
- Identify different spellings, e.g. u-e (*rule*), oo (*moon*), ue (*blue*), ew (*few*).
- Use a different colour for the phonemes and demonstrate horizontal joins.
- Write the beginning of a story using some of the suggested words, modelling joins.

Review
- Ask the children:
  - How many ways can you spell 'short' **oo**? (at least two ways)
  - How many ways can you spell 'long' **oo**? (at least three ways)
- Make lists of words for each spelling on a large sheet and in spelling logs for future reference.
- Homework review.
- Ask volunteers to spell the missing words on the PCM. Children spot and correct their own mistakes. Let the children swap sentences with a partner.

Follow-up homework
- Children write their own 'long' **oo** story using some of the brainstormed words.

Test dictation
- OB I would like a cat.
- A   On Monday we read a new book. The boy took my bike.
- B   On Tuesday it was very cool. The fish lives in the pool.
- C   Don't push the little boy over.

Snip-snap Word Chain
- The first child reads out a key word from the Y1/2 list, e.g. *again*. Everyone writes it on their dry-wipe board.
- The next child has to find a word beginning with previous word's last consonant, e.g. *next*.
- And so on… For words ending in *e*, remember to find the last consonant.

Snip-snap Remember these Words?
- Display or write up some words from the YR list, e.g. up, you, we, like, and.
- Cover one word; children write it on dry-wipe boards.
- Children keep their own scores – 'beat your best'.

3 Plural s

Objective for Unit 3
To use plural word ending s to support spelling

Part 1

You need Big Book page 6; dry-wipe boards or notebooks; Pupil's Book pages 6–7; PCM 3

Whole class
- Explain the objective – adding **s**.
- Look at the BBk page. Check that everyone knows the story of Noah's Ark, then read the rhyme together.
- Remind the children that the animals went in pairs – two of each kind.
- Teach the terms **singular** and **plural nouns** for *one thing* and *more than one thing*. Illustrate by adding **s**, e.g. *one elephant* becomes *two elephants*. Ask if children can hear the difference.
- Get Up and Go: ask volunteers to add **s** to each animal name in turn.
- Tell the children you're going to catch them out: what about *mouse*? Does *mouses* sound right? Does it look right?
- Remind them that there are always words which don't match the pattern!
- Show Me: call out a few singular cvc words (things that Noah might need to pack in the Ark, *e.g. cup, mug, pen*) which the children can spell and ask them to write the plural on dry-wipe boards in pairs.
- Write up *heads, shoulders, knees* and *toes*.
- Introduce the oddbods: *to, too, two* – see below.

Pupil activities
A: Label plural body parts.
B: List plurals in the classroom.
C: Investigation: children search their reading books and write down all the words that end in **s**. They sort them out into plural nouns / not plural nouns.

Extra challenge: Children work out why *scissors* and *trousers* are different. (plural in form but singular in meaning)

Review
- Show Me: as above with examples from Pupil's Books, e.g. *eye, ear, mouth, chair*.
- Point out that not all words ending in **s** are plural nouns. Ask group C to give some examples. Look at the title *Noah's Ark*.

Homework Children find animals for an animal alphabet.

Oddbod to, too, two
- Point out *two* in the BBk page title.
- Ask children to contribute other spellings: *to, too*.
- The tricky bit about these oddbods is deciding which one goes where! Use each one in a sentence, e.g. *two* by *two*. Did pigs go *too*?' Where did the Ark go *to*?

Snip-snap Plain Jane
- Call out a word.
- Children supply rhyming words; bonus if it has different spelling, e.g. *rule/cool*; *blue/do*; *cow/plough*; *grow/no*; *play/grey*.

Plural s

NLS objectives for Unit 3				
2.1.W2	2.1.W4	2.1.W7	2.1.W9	2.1.W12

Part 2

You need   Big Book page 7; dry-wipe boards or notebooks

Whole class
- Recap the objective.
- Look at the BBk page. Read or sing *Old Macdonald Had a Farm* together.
- Do the children think he really only had one cow? Look at the spelling sum: *a cow* + **s** = *some* and ask someone to show you how to change the word *cow*.
- Tell the children that you're going to add some more verses.
- Ask: what other animals might he have? (e.g. *pig**s***, *goat**s***, *horse**s***, *duck**s***, *chick**s***)
- Show Me: children write the spelling sums on dry-wipe boards. Scribe correct spellings on the board; emphasise handwriting joins, singing as you go!
- If they come up with exceptions, tell them there are quite a few catch-you-outs and they probably met some more in their homework.

Review
- Recap: you can add **s** to most nouns to make them plural but there are some catch-you-outs.
- Homework review.
- Look at some of the exceptions, e.g. *mouses*? *sheeps*? *wolfs*? Do they look and sound right? Has anyone found out the correct ending?

Follow-up homework
- Children collect plural nouns under headings and make lists for spelling logs, e.g. *animals*, *food*, *parts of body*, *in the garden*, *in the classroom*.

Test dictation
- OB   Ben has two brothers.
- A   Put your hands up high. We look with our eyes.
- B   The boys and girls are in the pool. Sam has three new books about cats.
- C   The girls put on their coats.

Snip-snap   Quickfire Catch-you-outs
- Try adding **s** to:
  - *house, mouse*;
  - *can, pan, van, man*;
  - *root, boot, foot*.
- Write up words and read together.
- Try *goose, wolf, child, tooth*.

Snip-snap   Noun Clues
- Tell the children you will be focusing on nouns from the key word list.
- Give a simple clue for each one, e.g. *something you can bounce*.
- Children race to guess and spell the words correctly on dry-wipe boards.
- Ask: who can make them into plurals?
- Words to use: *ball, cat, day, dog, bed, door, mum, dad, man, name, night, school, sister, tree*.

4 Adding ed

Objective for Unit 4
To use word ending ed to support spelling

Part 1

You need Big Book page 8; magnetic letters; letter fans for ed verbs; Pupil's Book pages 8–9; PCM 4

Whole class
- N.B. Focus on regular verbs that just add ed in the past tense.
- Focus on the BBk page. Read the words together: *walked*, *played*, *started* stretching out the words and emphasising the final sound.
- Ask the children to tell you what sounds they hear at the end – **t**, **d**, and **id**. Point out that the endings are all spelt the same – ed.
- How does the ed change the meaning of the word? Prompt by asking a child to walk to the door and say: He's walking to the door. Then ask: What did he do? Give me a sentence which tells me what he did. (E.g. He walked to the door.) Emphasise that ed verbs tell you about something that happened in the past.
- Get Up and Go: Write up some regular verbs. Ask volunteers to change them into the past tense by adding ed. Words to use: *play*, *want*, *like*, *help*, *jump*, *live*, *look*, *open*.
- Suggest some regular verbs ending in e, e.g. *like*, *live*, and discuss the rule that when a verb ends in e you only add d.
- If appropriate, include a catch-you-out at this point by spelling *stop*. Point out the need for doubling the consonant. Explain that the general rule is to double a single final consonant following a single vowel.
- Write up the following sentence, demonstrating the different ways ed is treated – *We jumped and hopped in the playground, then we needed a rest.*
- Introduce the oddbod: *people* – see below.

Pupil activities
A: Add ed to words and use in sentences.
B: Complete a poem using ed.
C: Make up sentences, using pairs of rhyming verbs, changing them to the past tense. Focusing on end sounds.

Think about...: Irregular verb *say*.

Review
- Recap: you can add ed to a verb to change it into the past tense.
  - The ed ending can sound different: **t**, **d**, **id** or **ed**.
  - If a verb ends in e then you only add d.

Homework Investigation of irregular verbs from the key word list.

Oddbod people
- Ask children to write the word. Share different spellings and identify problems.
- Identify the 'long' vowel phoneme **ee** and emphasise that this word has no family – it's unique!
- Ask children to suggest a mnemonic, e.g. by sounding out as *pe-op-le*.

Snip-snap Letter Fans (PiPs p. 28)
- Call out some ed verbs.
- Children listen and hold up the fan for the sound they hear – **t**, **d**, or **id**.
- Words to use: *played*, *wanted*, *walked*, *whistled*, *climbed*, *talked*, *started*, *fainted*, *called*, *kicked*.

Adding ed

NLS objectives for Unit 4
2.1.W2   2.1.W5   2.1.W7   2.1.W9   2.1.W12

Part 2 | **You need**   Big Book page 9; dry-wipe boards or notebooks; post-its

Whole class
- Read Nat's recount in the BBk.
- Get Up and Go: highlight the ed verb endings.
- Briefly discuss the catch-you-out *hurted*. Give other examples that small children often say (e.g. *drinked*, *goed*) because they are expecting the words to keep to the rules – to be *regular*. Emphasise that *hurt*, *drank* and *went* are all irregular. More about these in Year 3!
- Compose a short recount with the children about their weekend. Work on the spellings of ed verbs as you come to them.
  Ask: what letters should we add?
- Talk about diagonal handwriting joins as you write ed.

Review
- You can add ed to most verbs.
- The catch-you-out verbs are called *irregular* because they break the rules.
- Reiterate that the children will be learning more about the irregular ones in Year 3.
- Listen to some of group B's poems.
- Homework review.
- Ask children to share some of their ideas for sorting the key words and play Quickwrite with a few of the words (see PiPs p. 24).

Follow-up homework
- Children choose one set from their homework key word sort and make up sentences using the words.

Test dictation
- OB   Many people came to see the play.
- A   Tom pulled the dog back. She pushed her little sister.
- B   We walked to school today. My mum is called Pat.
- C   The man looked down from the moon.

Snip-snap   Rhyming Families (PiPs p. 34)
- Remind children of the **ee** sound in the oddbod *people*.
- Write *eat* on the board. Children suggest rhymes. (e.g. *street*, *sheet*, *meat*, *neat*)
- Write their words on post-its.
- Group the spellings by letter pattern.
- Talk about catch-you-out *Pete*!

Snip-snap   Spelling Soccer
- Two or more teams compete to spell key words from the homework list.
- Each correct spelling scores a goal.
- Differentiate words for individual players.

5 Adding ing

Objectives for Unit 5
To use word ending ing to support spelling; revise word endings s and ed

Part 1

You need Big Book page 10; dry-wipe boards or notebooks; Pupil's Book pages 10–11; PCM 5

Whole class
- Read the poem through together and enjoy the sounds.
- What do the children notice about the word endings? Highlight the examples of ing.
- Allocate a line to each pair and, using dry-wipe boards, ask them to write the stem verb for each ing ending, e.g. *rise, leap, sink*. Give line 1 to able spellers! Tell them the verb *writhe* in line 6.
- There are two catch-you-outs: *rising* and *writhing*. Can the children work out the rule for dropping the final e? Show them how odd the words would look with the two vowels next to each other.
- Write *hop* on the board and ask a volunteer to add ing. Point out pronunciation and meaning of *hope/hoping* (vowel phoneme **oa**); *hop/hopping* (vowel phoneme **o**).
- Get Up and Go: try some more examples – *run, stop, put*.
- Draw out the doubling rule for final consonants: when there is one vowel followed by one consonant, you double (exceptions are words ending in x and w, and some polysyllabic words, depending on stress).
- Compose a short piece titled *What's Going On?* about activities in the school, e.g. *The head teacher is talking to a parent. The secretary is counting up the dinner money.*
- Demonstrate handwriting joins for ing.
- Introduce the oddbod: *said* – see below.

Pupil activities
A: Add ing to regular words and complete sentences.
B: Add ing to regular and irregular words and write sentences.
C: Compose an ing poem using the Southey poem as a model.

Think about…: Doubling final consonant rule (Don't double if single vowel is followed by a consonant digraph.)

Review
- Recap: you double a final consonant that is preceded by a single vowel.

Homework
- Children sort a list of key words using their own categories.

Oddbod   said
- Notice that it rhymes with *bed* but has its own special spelling in the middle.
- Relate *say* and *said* to *pay* and *paid*.
- Look at the outline shape to remember there are two vowels in the middle.
- Shut eyes and 'photograph' it.
- Sky-write it.

Snip-snap   Key Word Tower
- Play in teams of two or more: teams can consult.
- Call out words from the key word list.
- A child from each team races to write the word on the board.
- If correct, draw the first block of tower round it; if wrong, wipe it off.
- The team with tallest tower at the end of the game wins.

| here |
| next |
| have |
| last |

10

Adding ing

NLS objectives for Unit 5				
2.1.W7	2.1.W8	2.1.W9	2.1.W10	2.1.W12

Part 2

You need   Big Book page 11; dry-wipe boards or notebooks

Whole class
- Recap on the rules for adding ing and ed: double a final consonant after a single vowel, drop final e, and watch out for catch-you-outs!
- Read the passage on the BBk page, pausing at each gap.
- Show Me: ask pairs to write the correct endings.
- Choose pairs with correct spellings to write them in the gaps.
- Look at each ending in turn, asking children to explain them.
- Compose another sentence and write up, emphasising joins, e.g. I _____ (hop) home and my sister was _____ (laugh) at me.

Review
- Ask children to sum up the rules.
- Ask: has anyone worked out the Extra challenge? Look briefly at verbs with single vowels and two consonants. Emphasise that you double a *single* consonant that follows a *single* vowel.
- Homework review.
- Discuss the irregular verbs children investigated for homework and start compiling a class list.

Follow-up homework
- Children collect examples of s, ed and ing endings from their reading books.

Test dictation
OB Jane said we could play with her.
A   The girl was shouting for help. Joe was calling me names.
B   Bob came running down the road. My dad is good at cooking.
C   The boys were hoping to come too.

Snip-snap   Word Sort – adding ing
- Use cards from Additional Literacy Support (p. 69) and instructions (p. 23).
- Sort the cards into pairs, e.g. *pat – patting*; *wish – wishing*.
- Sort them again into do or don't double the final consonant.
- Can children remind you of the rule?

Snip-snap   Word Shapes
- Display a list of selected key words with different outline shapes, e.g. *after, good, got*.
- Draw outline shapes on the board with divisions to indicate number of letters. 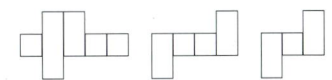
- Children take turns to find a matching word to place on an outline.
- Cover the words and spell them on dry-wipe boards.

6 Vowel phonemes ar and oy

Objective for Unit 6
To learn common spelling patterns for **ar** and **oy** (**oy** = PiPs **oi**)

Part 1

You need Big Book page 12; dry-wipe boards or notebooks; Pupil's Book pages 12–13; PCM 6

Whole class
- Say the sentence: *Last night it was dark after my father parked the car on the path by the yard*. Ask the children to spot the most common vowel sound.
- Ask the children to help you spell the sentence.
- Ask for examples of ways of spelling the phoneme **ar**, and write them on the board. N.B. Some British English speakers pronounce words such as *last*, *after* and *path* with a 'short' **a** as in *cat*, and some pronounce them with the **ar** sound. Discuss regional variations if appropriate, putting the words concerned in a separate column and asking if any of the children pronounce them differently.
- If helpful, compare the sound of **ar** with 'short' **a**, e.g. compare *am* with *arm*; *cat* with *cart*; *had* with *hard*.
- Read the star puzzles in the BBk together and ask children to fill in the answers. N.B. They are all examples of **ar** spelt **ar**. Children who pronounce *last* and *path* with the **ar** phoneme may need some further time spent on investigating words like these with **ar** spelt **a**.
- Discuss the catch-you-outs on the BBk page.
- Ask the children to suggest words that rhyme with them, e.g. *heart/part*, *half/laugh*, *calm/palm*. Look at whether the rhyming words are spelt the same, e.g. *palm/calm*, or are spelt differently, e.g. *heart/part*, *laugh/half*.
- Add any more spellings of **ar** to the list and write up a clue for one of the new words.
- Introduce the oddbod: *laugh* – see below.

Pupil activities
A: Complete the words *car*, *star*, *cart*, and *card*, then use other **ar** words in writing about the part.
B: Complete **ar** words from clues, then make up clues for other words.
C: Make up their own **ar** words using given letters.

Extra challenge: Make up more clues for **oy** words.

Review
- How many ways can **ar** be spelt? (at least two – **ar**, **a**, **ear**, **au**)
- Make lists of words for each spelling on a large sheet for future reference.

Homework Children use a list of the term's oddbod words to write a story.

Oddbod laugh 👁 👂
- Link it to other **ar** words (see above). The spelling **au** makes it an oddbod.
- Explore **gh** and the oddity of it sounding like **f**! Find other examples such as *cough*.
- Draw its outline shape (see Snip-snaps Unit 5) to establish the word visually.

Snip-snap ie investigation 💭 👂
- Ask children to provide rhymes for *try*, *night*, *like*, *line*.
- They then think of other words with the **ie** phoneme.
- Write the words on post-its. Sort into **y**, **i-e** and **igh** spellings.

Vowel phonemes ar and oy

NLS objectives for Unit 6				
2.1.W2	2.1.W3	2.1.W5	2.1.W9	2.1.W12

Part 2

You need Big Book page 13; dry-wipe boards or notebooks; letter fans with **oy** and **ar** phonemes

Whole class
- Read the sentences on the BBk page.
- Introduce phoneme spotting and spelling – which sound do they hear?
- Identify the different ways of spelling **oy** and write them on dry-wipe boards.
- Work out the rule. (at the end of a word or syllable **oy** is spelt with a *y*)
- To help children hear the syllables, clap them out, e.g. *roy/al, des/troys, an/noy/ing; noi/sy*.
- Compose a sentence with both **ar** and **oy** phonemes – it doesn't have to be sensible! e.g. *It's hard to boil a dark noise*.

Review
- Give some quickfire examples of **ar** and **oy** words and children hold up the correct phonemes in letter fans or show on dry-wipe boards.
- Practise handwriting joins for different letter strings in **ar** and **oy** phonemes.
- Homework review.
- Listen to some of the oddbod stories. Discuss mnemonics or other strategies for learning the oddbods.

Follow-up homework
- Children write an **ar** and **oy** story about characters called Mark and Joy.

Test dictation
- OB The big boy made us laugh.
- A Ron kicked the ball very far. On Monday we played in the park.
- B My little sister is very noisy. The dogs were digging in the brown soil.
- C We enjoy going to school.

Snip-snap   Full Circle
- Write *dark* on the board.
- Tell the children you're going to change one letter at a time to make a new word, until you come back to the word they started with.
- Children write on dry-wipe boards or volunteer to change each word, e.g. *park, part, cart, card, lard, lark,* and back to *dark*.
- Use an egg timer to hot up the pace.

Snip-snap   Word Caterpillar
- Play in two or more teams.
- Prepare sets of green paper circles with little legs on and one with a caterpillar face. Each group has one set.
- Call out key words one at a time. Everyone writes them on dry-wipe boards; a volunteer in each group writes them on paper circles.
- If correct, the circle is added to the caterpillar.
- If incorrect, the circle is added to a 'dead' caterpillar.
- The team with the longest 'living' caterpillar wins.

7 Vowel phoneme air

Objective for Unit 7
To learn the common spelling patterns for **air**

Part 1

You need Big Book page 14; dry-wipe boards or notebooks; letter fans with air, are, ear, ere; Pupil's Book pages 14–15; PCM 7

Whole class
- Read the poem in the BBk together, emphasising the sounds.
- Get Up and Go: ask the children to spot the **air** phoneme and underline the letters that spell it.
- Draw the children's attention to different spellings: air, are, ear.
- Discuss *scary* – find the stem word and remind children about dropping the *e*.
- Find the rhyming words for *scary* in the poem: *hairy, wary*.
- Focus on the oddbod words in the poem: *where, there* (see notes below).
- Hide the BBk page then read the poem again, stopping at **air** words. Children hold up fans showing the correct letter string.
- Get Up and Go: when you come to the oddbod words and to the catch-you-out *their*, children put up hands to write the word on the board.
- Write another short rhyme about the bear, e.g. *That bear doesn't care, if we tear our hair!*

Pupil activities
A: Write rhymes for pairs of air, ear, are words.
B: Find words whose endings are spelt the same as *chair, bear, share*.
C: Find **air** words, look at letter patterns, and complete short story with are words.

Extra challenge: Children think of words where the **air** phoneme comes at the beginning, using a dictionary to help. (The clue is *air – airmail*, etc.)

Review
- Ask children to contribute words from their lists.
- Ask them to tell you another, more common way of pronouncing *ear*. N.B. Children may contribute *heart* (from Unit 6) and words like *early, pearl*.
- Start a large wall list of words with the **air** sound, practising diagonal handwriting joins. Keep the sheet for future reference. Children can also write it in their spelling logs.

Homework Children fill the gaps in the poem *Beware the bear!*

Oddbods   there, where 👁 ✍
- Find the word within the word *here*.
- Link with the common theme of place.
- Make up quickfire sentences, e.g.
  He is over there.
  Where is she?
- Children practise joining *there, where* swiftly on dry-wipe boards.

Snip-snap   Homophones 🔊 💬
- Introduce **air** words that sound the same but have different spelling: *pear/pair, stare/stair, bear/bare, hair/hare*.
- Ask the children to make up sentences containing both words.
- Write them up and add 'crazy' pictures to illustrate the sentences.

14

Vowel phoneme air

NLS objectives for Unit 7
2.2.W1   2.2.W2   2.2.W6   2.2.W9   2.2.W14

Part 2

You need   Big Book page 15; dry-wipe boards or notebooks; six key word cards

Whole class
- Homework review.
- Ask the children to read the completed poem from their homework cloze exercise.
- Then turn to the BBk page. Read the poem *Milly and Billy* together with as much expression as possible.
- Get Up and Go: ask children to spot the **air** phoneme and underline the letter patterns.
- Work out the pattern of the poem. (each line end rhymes with an **air** word)
- Clap out the rhythm together.
- Compose more verses, e.g. *They bought a shirt they wouldn't wear./They got chased by a grizzly bear./They hurt themselves on a broken stair./They saw some shoes and bought a pair.*
- Ask the children to have a go at spelling each new **air** word on dry-wipe boards.

Review
- Ask: how many ways can you spell **air**? (at least three – *air*, *are*, *ear*) Make lists of words for each spelling on a large sheet for future reference.
- Remember the catch-you-outs, e.g. *there*, *where*.

Follow-up homework
- Children collect more **air** words from their reading books to add to the wall list.

Test dictation
OB *There* are lots of noisy people in our house.
A   On Saturday Dad took us to the *fair*. John pulled my *hair*.
B   Mum said I must not *stare*. They laughed and didn't *care*.
C   I saw a big *pear* tree in the park.

Snip-snap   Odd One Out Quiz
- Write up words with letter string *ear*, e.g. *wear, bear, near, pear.*
- Children write the odd one out on dry-wipe boards.
- Do the same with *ow*, e.g. *cow, now, mow, how.*
- Do the same with *oo*, e.g. *good, wood, food, hood.*
- Ask children to make up their own Odd One Out Quiz using the *our* letter string.

Snip-snap   Kim's Game
- Stick six key word cards to the board, e.g. *there, where, had, big, back, get.*
- Give children a minute to look at the words.
- Children close their eyes while you take a word away.
- Ask: who can remember *and* spell it?

8 Syllables

Objective for Unit 8
To discriminate syllables in speech and writing

Part 1

You need Big Book page 16; Pupil's Book 16–17; PCM 8

Whole class
- Teach the word *syllable* – a block of sound that has one 'beat' in a word. N.B. There is often more than one possible way of syllabifying a word. The best rule to follow is that each syllable should be pronounceable on its own – so *cap/tain* rather than *ca/ptain*.
- Read the *Syllable School register* on the BBk page, helping the children to separate the syllables to read the names.
- Tap out the syllables in each name and agree the number.
- Count and clap out syllables in children's own names.
- Then play Syllable Sort. Ask children to stand in different corners of the room according to the number of syllables in their name.
- Chant the sets of names, emphasising the rhythms (stressed syllables).
- Explain that breaking words into syllables can help with reading and spelling words. Work through an example, e.g. *Car/o/line Cat/er/pill/ar*, looking for words within words.
- Introduce the oddbod: *another* – see below.
- If time, make up some more names for the *Syllable School register*.

Pupil activities
A: Sort animal names into syllable sets.
B: Sort clothes into syllable sets and add more.
C: Write lists of food items and sort them into syllable sets.

Extra challenge: Think of an animal name with more than four syllables.

Review
- Ask children to explain the meaning of *syllable*.
- Ask a volunteer who has had a go at the extra challenge to demonstrate how to separate *hippopotamus* into syllables.

Homework Children count the number of syllables in each word of a poem.

Oddbod another
- Pronounce the word, emphasising the syllables: *an/oth/er*.
- Then look for words within the word: (*an, no, the, her, not*).

Snip-snap Spelling Long Words
- With children's help, choose some long words, e.g. *dinosaur, Wednesday, library*, or any other topic words the children find tricky.
- Ask the children to divide them up into syllables.
- Say, study and write each syllable.
- Write the word in the air.

Syllables

NLS objectives for Unit 8				
2.2.W5	2.2.W6	2.2.W9	2.2.W10	2.2.W14

Part 2 | **You need** | Big Book page 17; dry-wipe boards or notebooks

Whole class
- Read the syllable poems together. What do the children notice about them? Can they explain why they are called *syllable poems*?
- Clap and count the syllables together.
- Look at the pattern of the poems – an animal's name, then a verb, then a word describing the verb, ending in *ly* (an adverb). Each line begins with the same letter.
- Read the instructions then compose your own syllable poems e.g. *cat/crouches/carefully*.

Review
- Read the new syllable poems together, clapping the syllables.
- Show syllable breaks in the words and emphasise how to find words within words to help with spelling.
- Homework review.
- Discuss the results of the syllable counting.

Follow-up homework
- Children make a list of topic words. You can share word lists in class and write words on cards, building up a collection. Later on you can use them for a variety of activities, including listing words in syllable sets, alphabetical order, or phoneme sorts.

Test dictation
OB I went home with Jo and another boy.
A   The cow was black and white. I stared at the blue butterfly.
B   Today I put on my red jumper. Then I put on my yellow socks.
C   You should have a scarf when it is cool.

Snip-snap   Can't Catch Me
- Display a list of about ten one- and two-syllable key words.
- Clap either one or two syllables.
- Children call out any word on the list with the same number of syllables.
- Cover the word before the children spell it on dry-wipe boards.

Snip-snap   Sandwich Fillings
- Provide the children with initial and final consonants, e.g. b-t; h-l. Ask them to put in the vowel phoneme 'filling' to spell as many words as possible, e.g. *beat, boat, beet, bait, boot; hill, hall, hail, haul, heal*.
- Practise handwriting joins on the board and on dry-wipe boards.

9 Vowel phoneme er

Objective for Unit 9

To learn the common spelling patterns for the vowel phoneme **er** (**er** = PiPs **er** and **ur**)

Part 1

You need Big Book page 18; dry-wipe boards or notebooks; Pupil's Book pages 18–19; PCM 9

Whole class
- Look at the word list on the BBk page and read it aloud together.
- Ask: who can spot which phoneme the words have in common?
- Get Up and Go: volunteers come up to underline the **er** phoneme.
- Time Out: ask the children to write the three different spellings for the phoneme **er** on their dry-wipe boards. (ir, ur, er)
- Use the chart in the BBk – ir, ur, er – and sort the words into groups together.
- Add more words to each group.
- Look at the picture together and identify the words illustrated.
- Compose a silly sentence as a caption for the illustration, e.g. *a bird in a fur and turkey in a skirt were whirling over the kerb by the church.*
- Introduce the oddbod: *were* – see below.

Pupil activities
A: Write and illustrate silly sentences from given words.
B: As A, but children use their own words and use a dictionary to check spelling.
C: Complete a story using their own **er** words.

Extra challenge: Think of **er** words spelt *or* or *ear*.

Review
- Ask: how many ways of spelling **er**? (at least three – ir, ur, er). Make lists of words for each spelling on a large sheet for future reference.
- Write catch-you-out **or** words on the board, e.g. *worm, word, work*. What do they have in common? (they all begin with w)
- Write up other catch-you-outs: *learn, earn, early*. (N.B. In some dialects these words are pronounced with a different phoneme.)
- Make a special catch-you-out list for the wall.

Homework Crossword with **er** words.

Oddbod were
- Another catch-you-out **er** word – it sounds like *wurr*.
- The letter string *ere* links the word with *here, there, where.*
- Write in joined-up handwriting, modelling diagonal and horizontal joins.
- Children do the same without looking at your version.

Snip-snap Spelling Race
- Work in teams or pairs.
- The object is to find and spell as many **er** words as possible.
- The team with most words correctly spelt wins.
- Use dictionaries to check words.

Vowel phoneme er

NLS objectives for Unit 9
2.2.W2   2.2.W6   2.2.W9   2.2.W13   2.2.W14

Part 2

You need Big Book page 19; dry-wipe boards or notebooks; key word card sets

Whole class
- Look briefly at the BBk page 19 and ask the children to point to a word where er comes at the end (*painter*).
- Say the word and ask the children to listen carefully to the sounds. Can they hear that the ur and er sound slightly different? Explain that at the end of a word er is sometimes pronounced a bit differently – it can sound like **u**.
- Time Out: children think of words ending in er and write on dry-wipe boards.
- Turn to the BBk page 19. Ask the children to suggest words for each occupation illustrated. (*farmer, painter, writer, skateboarder, builder*) Write them on the board.
- Get Up and Go: ask them to find the word within each word which describes what the person does – the verb – and underline it on the board. N.B. Point out the single e in *writer*.
- Turn back to the BBk and ask children to supply er words for the verbs at the bottom of the page. Introduce catch-you-outs, e.g. double m in *swimmer* (N.B. Doubling will be a focus in Year 3 term 1); no double e to turn *bake* into *baker* or *bike* into *biker*.
- Write up a sentence to demonstrate the changes from verb to noun, e.g. '*I only like to bake,' said the baker.*

Review
- Ask: how many ways can you spell er? (there are three main ways – ir, ur, er) Make lists of words for each spelling on a large sheet for future reference.
- Remember the catch-you-outs or and ear.
- Homework review.
- Check how many different spellings of er children found in the crossword.

Follow-up homework
- Children collect more occupation er words for spelling logs notebooks.

Test dictation
- OB The boys were cooking some food.
- A   The bird was in the tree. Bob ran and came third.
- B   Her brother has fair hair. We will come back to school next term.
- C   My cat loves to purr.

Snip-snap Magnetic Multiplication
- Start with a simple word from YR key word list, e.g. *at*.
- Explain that if you know how to spell at you can spell lots of other words too.
- Generate rhymes, e.g. *bat, cat, fat*, going through the alphabet and demonstrating the cvc pattern.
- Challenge children to find more words using consonant clusters, e.g. th, sp, spr, fl, br, sc.

Snip-snap Key Word Sentence Race
- Make a set of cards from the key word list.
- Give pairs of children four cards each.
- Children race to compose a sentence using all the words.
- The first pair says their sentence and spells the key words.

19

10 Vowel phoneme or

Objective for Unit 10

To learn the common spelling patterns for the vowel phoneme **or**
N.B. Pronunciation of this phoneme varies regionally. PiPs divides the **or** phoneme into **or** (as in *torn*, *door*, *warn*) and **au** (as in *haul*, *law*, *call*). Some children will pronounce these two phonemes distinctly and, in recognition of this, the unit follows this distinction, focusing first on **or** then on **au**.

Part 1

You need Big Book page 20; dry-wipe boards or notebooks; Pupil's Book 20–21; PCM 10

Whole class
- Look at the BBk page and read the word list together.
- Identify the rhyming words.
- Can children identify the common letter pattern? (**or**)
- Look at the illustration together and spot the words. Compose a silly sentence as a caption for the illustration, e.g. *A dinosaur with a sore forehead fell by the door at number four.*
- In pairs, ask children to think of a rhyming word (same sound, same final letter pattern) for *sore* (e.g. *store*), *door* (e.g. *floor*) and *four* (e.g. *pour*).
- Make a list of the different spellings of **or**. Emphasise again that the most common is **or** but when the phoneme comes at the end of the word the spelling can be **ore** or **oor** or **our**. Mention the catch-you-out *war* (as in *warm*).
- Introduce the oddbod: *door* – see below.

Pupil activities
A: Continue a silly story from given words.
B: As A but children use their own words.
C: Sorting own **or** words according to letter pattern.

Extra challenge: Investigate the spelling of **or** at the beginning of words.

Review
- Ask: how many ways can you spell the **or** phoneme? (at least four – see below). Can children tell you where they are most likely to find the different spellings, e.g. **or** (middle of word); **ore**, **oor**, **our** (end)?

Homework Children investigate the sound **or** at the end of words.

Oddbod door
- Learn the word as an example of the **or** phoneme (spelt the same as *floor*).
- It sounds like *dor*.
- Sky-write, emphasising the double **o** and demonstrating horizontal joins.

Snip-snap Phoneme Frame (PiPs p. 22)
- Draw three boxes on the board.
- Say the word *born* and write it on the board.
- Ask children to identify the first phoneme and its letter **b**.
- Write the letters in the first box of frame.
- Continue with **or** and **n**. Repeat with *fork*, *cord*, *storm*.

20

Vowel phoneme or

NLS objectives for Unit 10				
2.2.W2	2.2.W6	2.2.W9	2.2.W13	2.2.W14

Part 2   **You need**   Big Book page 21; dry-wipe boards or notebooks

Whole class
- Look at the BBk page. Read the title and the report out loud.
- Ask the children what they notice about the title *Animal Sports Report*. Underline the or spelling.
- Get Up and Go: ask the children to identify and underline other words with the **or** phoneme. Did they spot the catch-you-out ar spelling in *towards*?
- Now focus on the **au** phoneme, introducing it as appropriate, depending upon whether children pronounce, e.g. *source* and *sauce*, with different phonemes. Ask: can you spot other words with a very similar sound or different vowel sound?
- Get Up and Go: ask children to underline (in a different colour if appropriate) the letter patterns that spell the **au** phoneme e.g. aw, au, a, al.
- Investigate some of the catch-you-outs, e.g. al in *walk* where l is silent; silent gh in *caught*. (N.B. Children will have learnt this word for homework.) Ask children for other examples of both spellings (e.g. *taught*, *talk*).
- If time, compose another short animal sports report using the word and picture prompts on the BBk page, e.g. *Four tall horses walked across the lawn on a warm day and jumped the short wall*.

Review
- Recap on the different spelling patterns for **au**. Brainstorm words for each spelling pattern and write under separate headings.
- Homework review.
- Write up the lists and add new or words thought of by the children.

Follow-up homework
- Children illustrate **or**/**au** words on cards for a classroom word mobile, e.g. *door, core, jaw*. Alternatively, children write another short sports report, using as many **or**/**au** words as possible.

Test dictation
- OB   Help me close the door.
- A   My brother is very tall. Chris jumped off the wall.
- B   The cat hurt me with her claw. Dad wore a green tie.
- C   The scary dog was caught.

Snip-snap   Full Circle (PiPs p. 29)
- Write *born* on the board.
- Tell the children they're going to change one letter at a time to make a new word until they come full circle back to the word they started with.
- Children write on dry-wipe boards to change each word, e.g. *cord, ford, fort, port, pork, fork, stork, storm, torn*, and back to *born*.

Snip-snap   Key Word Battle
- Play in two teams, keeping up a brisk pace.
- One team calls out a key word from a selected list.
- A member of the other team spells the word on a dry-wipe board. (The team can consult.)
- The speller scores a point for the correct spelling but is 'out' if incorrect.
- Swap sides when the team is out, or after an agreed length of time.

11 Digraphs wh ch ph and f phoneme

> **Objective for Unit 11**
>
> To spell words with the digraphs wh, ph, ch
> N.B. In some dialects, the initial sound of *where*, etc. is phonemically different from the initial sound of *wake*, being pronounced with an 'aspirated' w.

Part 1

You need Big Book page 22; dry-wipe boards or notebooks; Pupil's Book pages 22–23; PCM 11

Whole class
- Remind children about words with two consonants together which make one sound, e.g. sh, ch, th, and write examples on the board, e.g. *shut, church, the, dash, peach, bath*. Ask children to ring the digraphs. Point out that they all have h in them.
- Look at the picture and wh words on the BBk page. Ask the children to spot what the words have in common. (two consonants together making one sound)
- Identify the words illustrated and write them on the board.
- Explain that some words start with two consonants but you can only hear one of them.
- Get Up and Go: ask children to identify the phoneme they can hear at the beginning of each word and then to circle the silent h.
- Point out that there are two ways of pronouncing ch. Children write examples on dry-wipe boards, practising handwriting joins, e.g. *chess, Christmas*.
- Brainstorm some more examples of words with the sound ch (as in *chess*), e.g. *chip, challenge, beach*. Write a short sentence using the words, e.g. *Playing chess on the beach, while eating chips is a challenge.*
- Introduce the oddbod: *who* – see below.

Pupil activities
- A: Learn wh question words.
- B: Make up questions with wh words to find out about someone using speech bubbles.
- C: Use a dictionary to find wh and ph words.

Extra challenge: Use a dictionary to find some ch words and sort them according to sound.

Review
- Recap consonant phonemes with silent h. List *who, what, where, why, when*. Can the children suggest others?

Homework
Explain what a consonant pair is and give an example – th. Explain also that some letters never go with h, e.g. fh, lh. Children then investigate consonants which can pair with h.

Oddbod who 👁 🎵 😊
- Emphasise wh at beginning (but the sound is h).
- Relate it to rhyming words *do/to*.
- Practise writing swiftly on dry-wipe boards.

Snip-snap Question Time 👁 🎵
- Choose a child to be the celebrity of the day.
- Children write questions on dry-wipe boards, starting with a wh word.
- Children take it in turns to be interviewed.

Digraphs wh ch ph and f phoneme

NLS objectives for Unit 11
2.2.W3   2.2.W6   2.2.W9   2.2.W13   2.1.W14

Part 2

You need Big Book page 23; dry-wipe boards or notebooks; letter fans with f, ff, ph (optional)

Whole class
- Help the children to read aloud together the words in the BBk – some tricky words here.
- Ask them to find what sound the words have in common. (**f**)
- Sort the words under the headings on the BBk page.
- Can children find any words to add under each heading? Prompt if necessary, e.g. *thief*, *photo*, *cliff*, *cough*. Try spelling them on dry-wipe boards – which way looks right?
- Get Up and Go: children add the words to the BBk page.
- Which letters or consonant pairs can come at the beginning of words? (all except ff and gh)
- Brainstorm some more words spelt with ph.
- Say some words: *stuff*, *photo*, *rough*, *father* and ask the children to hold up the correct letters from their fans, or try them out on dry-wipe boards.
- Write up a sentence using some of the words, e.g. *The thief took the stuff, but we took a photo of her.*

Review
- Recap consonant combinations wh, ph, ch with examples.
- Homework review.
- List all the combinations with h from the investigation.
- Start a word wall so that children can add to the wh, p, ch collections (and you could include th and sh).

Follow-up homework
- Children compose their own sentences using this week's words to learn.

Test dictation
- OB Who started to laugh first?
- A   When did you come home? What is your last name?
- B   Christmas is in December. Jill wanted to play chess.
- C   An elephant can't jump.

Snip-snap Name Sounds
- Write **Christopher** on the board highlighting Ch and ph.
- Children identify the focal sounds.
- Brainstorm girls' and boys' names with the same **ch**, **ph** sounds, e.g. *Philip*, *Sophie*, *Nicholas*, *Stephen*, *Chloë*, *Michael*.

Snip-snap Inflectional Endings
- Choose a set of key word cards, including several verbs, e.g. *walk*, *help*, *laugh*.
- Make a set of inflectional ending cards, e.g. ed, s, ing, er.
- Display the cards and invite children to use both sets to make a new word.

23

12 Negative prefixes and opposites

> **Objective for Unit 12**
> To spell words with common prefixes to indicate the negative.

Part 1

You need Big Book page 24; dry-wipe boards or notebooks; Pupil's Book pages 24–25; PCM 12

Whole class
- Introduce the term *prefix* and explain that *prefixes* are letter strings which you put in front of a word to change its meaning.
- Introduce the prefix un and write it on the board. Then write *happy*.
- Ask the children to put the prefix un in front of the word *happy*, writing the new word on dry-wipe boards. How has the prefix changed the meaning? Repeat with *fair*.
- Can the children deduce the meaning of un? (not, the reverse or do the opposite of something, as in *undo*) Point out that dis is another prefix meaning 'not', e.g. *disagree*.
- Look at the BBk page. Help the children to understand how the meaning machine works. Try adding the prefixes un and dis to the root words *tidy, pack, cover, agree, appear, kind, obey*.
- Make a list of the root words and their negatives, and discuss meanings: *untidy, unkind, unpack, uncover, discover, disagree, disappear, disobey*.
- Identify the root which can use both prefixes *cover*.
- Some other prefixes mean 'not' as well: ask the children to work out which part of the word is the prefix in *impossible* and *misbehave*.
- Introduce the oddbod: *once* – see below.

Pupil activities
A: Make words with the meaning machine: un + *do, happy, safe, fair, tie*.
B: Cloze text: children add the prefix un or dis.
C: Children add the prefix un, mis or dis to *usual, appear, understand, take* and write the meanings of the new words.

Think about…: Look for and list prefixes used in own writing.

Review
- Recap prefixes meaning 'not': un, dis, mis.

Homework
Children use the list of oddbods from the term to write a story.

Oddbod once
- Ask the children to think of another word that looks and sounds rather like *once*. (*one*)
- Ask the children to spell the word *one*. Then link it to *once*. (*one time*)
- Work out a mnemonic, e.g. *one with the c in the middle*.

Snip-snap Prefix Family
- Write the word *misfortune* on the board.
- Point out the root *fortune* as a word within a word. (Discuss the meaning of the word, linking it to stories where characters go off to seek their fortune.)
- Identify the prefix mis and guess the meaning. (*bad* or *badly*).

Negative prefixes and opposites

NLS objectives for Unit 12			
2.2.W6	2.2.W8	2.2.W9	2.1.W14

Part 2 | **You need** Big Book page 25; dry-wipe boards or notebooks

Whole class
- Recap: *unhappy* is the opposite of *happy*.
- What other word could you use? (e.g. *sad*)
- Do the same with *unkind* (e.g. *cruel*) and *untidy* (e.g. *messy*).
- Look at the sentences on the BBk page and identify the words to change. (e.g. *tall, running, quickly*)
- Write up opposites for each one, e.g. *short, walking, slowly*.
- Show Me: check meanings and spellings.
- Children work in pairs writing the opposites for other sentences on dry-wipe boards.
- Get Up and Go: choose children to change the sentences in the BBk.

Review
- Ask children to identify at least two prefixes meaning 'not' and give examples.
- Point out that you can add *dis* and *mis* to *trust* to make two new words with the same meaning.
- Homework review.
- Listen to some of the oddbod stories. Discuss mnemonics or other strategies for learning the oddbods.

Follow-up homework
- Children find examples of negative words using other prefixes: *in, ir,* and *non*.

Test dictation
- OB Once I saw a big brown bear.
- A Your brother is a very unkind boy. The girl in the photo looked unhappy.
- B My sister and I disagree all the time. Tim made a mistake.
- C Some people misbehave at school.

Snip-snap   Opposites
- Play in teams.
- Choose words which have opposites in the key word list, e.g. *up* (*down*), *hate* (*love*), *on* (*off*), *come* (*go*), *day* (*night*), *small* (*big*), *in* (*out*), *before* (*after*), *cry* (*laugh*), *give* (*take*), *forward* (*back*), *don't* (*do*), *less* (*more*), *bad* (*good*).
- Write the first word on the board.
- The first team to call out the opposite and spell it correctly wins the point.

Snip-snap   Key Word Hunt
- Write a short list of high-frequency key words on the board, e.g. *always, also, any, before, there, first*.
- Give pairs of children photocopies of a page from a magazine or newspaper and a pen.
- Children ring words on the list: highest number wins. (Set a time limit.)

13 Same spelling pattern, different sounds

Objective for Unit 13
To investigate words which have the same spelling pattern but different sounds.

Part 1

You need Big Book page 26; dry-wipe boards or notebooks; Pupil's Book pages 26–27; PCM 13

Whole class
- Write the word *bow* on the board. Ask the children to read it aloud.
- Help them to realise that there are two ways of pronouncing it and two different meanings.
- Ask: can you think of any other words with the letter string ow? Write them on dry-wipe boards. (e.g. *cow, now, tow, sow, bow, row*)
- Show Me: notice the different sounds. (Remember that *sow, bow* and *row* can be pronounced in two different ways.)
- Recap: sometimes the same letter pattern can sound different.
- Look at the BBk page. Read the speech bubbles aloud. Ask children to identify the odd one out in each set. (*row, here, good, home, move*)
- Demonstrate handwriting joins for the letter strings ow, ere, oo, ome, ove.
- Write a sentence using some of the words, e.g. *That cow is so slow*.
- Introduce the oddbods: *some* and *come* – see below.

Pupil activities
A: Children sort words with the same spelling but different sounds (*no, go, so, to, who, do*) and make up a speech bubble.
B: As A (*our, your, hour, four, pour, sour*).
C: As A but making up a short poem (*bone, lone, one, done, stone, phone*).

Extra challenge: Children think of two words that are spelt with the same letter pattern (one) but rhyme with *on*.

Review
- Ask children to read out examples from their independent work.

Homework
Children investigate letter pattern ear and associated phonemes.

Oddbod some, come
- Write *some, home, come* on the board. Ask which is the odd one out? (*home*)
- Focus on the ome pattern: *some, come, home*.
- Look at the compound words *sometime, something, somewhere, somehow*.
- Practise writing with horizontal and diagonal handwriting joins.
- Sky-write the word.

Snip-snap Phoneme Snap
- Make word cards with several groups of letter patterns. Have some words spelt the same that rhyme and some spelt the same but not rhyming. e.g. *bar, car, war, star, far, tar, warm, farm, harm, calm, word, sword, bird*.
- Hold the cards up one at a time.
- The first child to call 'Snap!' gets the rhyming pair.

Same spelling pattern, different sounds

NLS objectives for Unit 13
2.3.W6   2.3.W8   2.3.W9   2.3.W12

Part 2

You need   Big Book page 27; dry-wipe boards or notebooks

Whole class
- Read the tongue twisters in the BBk together as fast as you can.
- Ask the children to write the common letter strings *oth* and *ow* on dry-wipe boards. Identify the different sounds represented by each, e.g. *oth* – *moth*, *mother*, *both*; *ow* – *cow*, *show* and practise pronouncing them.
- Write the words *bone, lone, one, done, stone, phone*, on the board.
- Ask the children to read the words aloud.
- Compose another tongue twister e.g. *"Well done!" said the bone to the stone one day*.
- Ask if anyone found an answer to the challenge – words spelt with the letter pattern *one* but rhyming with *on*? Add *shone* and *gone* (and maybe *scone*!) to the tongue twister.
- Practise saying the completed tongue twister together.

Review
- Ask for examples of 'same spelling, different sound' from homework.
- Ask the children to think of another letter string which can be pronounced differently, and make up similar questions to ask each other, e.g. *What word looks like* ove *but sounds like* oove?

Follow-up homework
- Children find more words that are spelt the same but sound different for a class display.

Test dictation
- OB   Some people don't enjoy Christmas.
- A   The school play was very good. Mum cooked some food for us.
- B   Is that your cat out there? There are four birds in the tree.
- C   My little brother is five now.

Snip-snap   Guess the Subject
- Read out words from the subject vocabulary (see reference pages in Pupil's Book).
- Children guess the topic or subject and spell the word.

Snip-snap   Split Digraphs (PiPs p. 36)
- Say the word *tie* and ask children to spell it on dry-wipe boards.
- Identify the phoneme **ie**.
- Ask a child to make *tie* into *time*.
- Point out that even though the *i* and *e* have been split, they still make the same sound – draw a line linking them together.
- Carry on making other words, e.g. *crime, lime, like, line, pine, pie*.

14 Vowel phoneme *ear*

> **Objective for Unit 14**
> To spell and read the phoneme **ear**

Part 1

You need Big Book page 28; dry-wipe boards or notebooks; Pupil's Book pages 28–29; PCM 14

Whole class
- Look at the word family lists on the BBk page.
- Explain the Venn diagram. Look at the example given in each section: words that are spelt the same; words that sound the same; words that belong in both sections because they are spelt the same *and* sound the same.
- Get Up and Go: read out each word in turn and ask a volunteer to write it in the right section.
- Write up rhymes using words from each group, e.g. *I can hear, loud and clear*.
- Introduce the oddbods: *here, hear* – see below.

Pupil activities
A: Solve an **ear** words puzzle (cloze activity).
B: Add more words and make up rhymes with the words *gear, bear, dear, here, hear, cheer*.
C: Sort the words *spear, clear, steer, here, sneer, wear*. Add more words.

Think about...: Think of other spellings of the phoneme **ear**.

Review
- Recap on the **ear** phoneme and exceptions to the ear spelling. (eer, ere)
- Point out that once you know how to spell one word in the family, you can spell many more by just changing a letter, e.g. *hear, fear, near*.

Homework Children write down in 15 minutes as many words as they think they can spell correctly.

Oddbod   here, hear
- Children may confuse the spelling of these two words, so it is helpful to teach *hear* with the rest of the ear letter string family.
- Link *here* with related 'place' word *there*.
- Think of a helpful mnemonic, e.g. *Can you hear the ear sound here?*

Snip-snap   Hear ear
- Start with everyone standing up.
- Write ear on the board.
- Tell children that they should sit down when they hear the phoneme **ear**.
- Say any word which contains the ear letter string, e.g. *ear, bear, year, fear, wear, tear* (crying), *tear* (ripping), *near, spear, clear*.
- To make it harder, you could vary the rule – children sit down if they think a word is <u>spelt</u> with ear. Intersperse with words which sound the same but are spelt differently, e.g. *there, fair, care, hair, here, pier, steer*.

Vowel phoneme ear

NLS objectives for Unit 14					
2.3.W1	2.3.W3	2.3.W4	2.3.W8	2.3.W11	2.3.W12

Part 2 | You need Big Book page 29

Whole class
- Read the Nearly and Really Rhymes on the BBk page aloud together.
- Ask the children to explain the title. Then ask them to find the non-rhyming words.
- Compose some 'really rhymes' lines to replace the 'nearly rhymes', e.g. the easiest solution for the first one is to change *bear* to *deer*! Other possibilities would be *Oh dear, oh dear* and *I'll get my gear*.
- Cross out and insert the new words on the BBk page.
- Write out a finished rhyme on the board, demonstrating diagonal handwriting joins for ear and eer.

Review
- Brainstorm alternative ways of spelling **ear** (eer, ere, ier).
- Emphasise that ear is the most common and therefore the most likely spelling.
- Homework review.
- Discuss, reminding children of useful strategies – words within words, rhyming words, etc. Help the least confident children to discover how much they know.

Follow-up homework
- Children make up sentences with **ear** words.

Test dictation
- OB The old lady can't hear what you say.
- A   That elephant has a big ear. Our house is near my school.
- B   The girls and boys began to cheer. I will take my PE gear to school.
- C   Mum can steer the car down the road.

Snip-snap Rhyme Ball
- Play with children sitting close together or spaced out in the hall.
- Say a word as you throw the ball to a child.
- The child says a rhyming word before throwing the ball back.
- Use **ear** words to reinforce discrimination of the sound.
- Every now and then, stop and spell a word!

Snip-snap Jumbly
- Choose key words starting with same letter of the alphabet, e.g. b.
- Write jumbled words on the board, e.g. *nebe* (been), *oby* (boy), *albl* (ball).
- Tell the children what the first letter will be.
- Show the children how to write the letters in a circle to help them work out the word.
- Highlight likely letter combinations, e.g. *It can't be n after b.*

29

15 Adding suffix ly

Objective for Unit 15

To spell words with common suffixes ful and ly

Part 1

You need Big Book page 30; Pupil's Book pages 30–31; PCM 15

Whole class
- Remind children of what a *prefix* is – letter strings you fix in front of a word to change its meaning (see Unit 12).
- Remind them of how they added ed and ing to words (Units 4 and 5). Introduce the term *suffix* – letter strings you fix at the end of a word to change its meaning.
- Write the word *slow* on the board. Then walk very slowly and deliberately across the room. Ask the children to describe how you're walking. (*slowly*)
- Add ly to the word *slow* on the board using a different colour for the suffix.
- Walk quickly and repeat the question. (*quickly*) (Deal with *fast* and *fastly* if necessary, explaining that you can't always make a word by adding ly.)
- Look at the BBk page and read the words in the column first. Draw lines to join the words to the pictures.
- Get Up and Go: ask children to add ly to each word.
- Read the words in the last two columns and ask: what have they got in common? (they all end in y). Explain that if the word ends in y you change it to i before adding ly.
- Demonstrate with *happy* using two children (one child changes the y to i and the other adds ly). Change the remaining words in the same way.
- Introduce the oddbod: *because* – see below.

Pupil activities
A: Add ly to given words and write sentences about Sammy Snail.
B: Add ly to given words, including some with y and use them to write about themselves.
C: Look at ily endings. Think of more examples and complete writing.

Think about...: Guess what happens to *gentle* if you add ly.

Review
- Recap: a suffix goes at the end of a word and changes its meaning.
- Introduce suffix ful in preparation for homework by adding it to *thank*.
- Discuss the meaning – 'full of thanks'.

Homework Suffix ful investigation.

Oddbod because
- The best way to learn this tricky oddbod is to make up a mnemonic, e.g. **b**ig **e**lephants **c**an **a**lways **u**nderstand **s**mall **e**lephants.
- Look for words within the word.

Snip-snap Opposite Meanings
- Write *care* on the board.
- Ask a child to add a ful letter card.
- Give the next child a less letter card to change the word.
- Discuss the meaning, reminding children of work on opposites.
- Do the same with *thank*, *help*, *hope*, *harm*.

Adding suffix ly

NLS objectives for Unit 15				
2.3.W6	2.3.W7	2.3.W8	2.3.W11	2.3.W12

Part 2 | **You need** Big Book page 31; dry-wipe boards or notebooks

Whole class
- Read the poem in the BBk together.
- Look at the words ending in ly and identify the root word *nice*.
- Use the poem as a model to write about other kinds of rain the children have experienced.
- Brainstorm ly words for the first line, e.g. *softly, gently, kindly, fiercely, wildly, coldly*.
- Compose the rest of the poem, e.g. *fiercely . . . in the forest/The rain beats the trees like a giant*.
- Encourage the children to compose their own verses, each one starting with an adverb.

Review
- Ask the children to define *suffix* and give examples.
- Homework review.
- Start a list of words with ful endings.
- Look briefly at how the y changes to i, as it does when you add ly.

Follow-up homework
- Children write simple two-line ly poems e.g. *Gently/The mother rocked her little baby./Loudly/The train thundered through the station.*

Test dictation
- OB I love my sister because she is cheerful.
- A The tall man laughed loudly. My big brother ran slowly.
- B Polly jumped over the wall easily. The cat sat there calmly.
- C At school I am very helpful.

Snip-snap The Adverb Game
- Take it in turns to act out 'I walked', adding different ly words, e.g. I walked... *slowly, quickly, nervously, neatly*.
- Others guess the adverb and spell it on dry-wipe boards.

Snip-snap Key Word Clues
- Give simple oral clues to words from the high frequency list, e.g. the opposite of before. (*after*)
- In pairs, children guess the word and spell it on dry-wipe boards – remind them to whisper!
- The first pair to show the correct spelling gives the next clue.

16 ea and ear

Objective for Unit 16
To spell and read the digraph *ea*, and letter pattern *ear*

Part 1

You need Big Book page 32; dry-wipe boards or notebooks; Pupil's Book pages 32–33; PCM 16

Whole class
- Read the words on the BBK page: *Jean, Dean, tea, bread, spread, peas, beans, instead, please, head, read.*
- Point out the two pronunciations and meanings for *read*. (You could act this out: open a book and read – then close the book.)
- Get Up and Go: invite children to come out and underline the 'long' and 'short' vowel phoneme in different colours.
- Count up how many are *ee* phonemes and how many are 'short' *e* phonemes.
- Look at the *d* endings of 'short' *e* words.
- Make up a story using the words, e.g. *Jean had beans and bread for tea*. Encourage the children to be far-fetched – it will help the spellings to stick!
- Introduce the oddbod: *after* – see below.

Pupil activities
A: Sort given *ea* words according to sound and think of own.
B: Think of *ea* words and sort as above. Write sentences.
C: Write short rhymes using *ea* words.

Extra challenge: Think of words that have not come up in the whole class session that rhyme with *head* but are not spelt with *ea*. (e.g. *bed*)

Review
- Recap: the vowel phoneme *e* can be spelt *ea*. Ask children for examples.
- What are the other ways of spelling the sound? Did anyone solve the Extra challenge? (e.g. *bed, said*)

Homework *ead* and *eat* investigations.

Oddbod after
- Divide into *aft/er*: first part rhymes with *daft*; *er* is a common suffix. (Remind children of the words they looked at in Unit 9, e.g. *teacher*.)
- Practise writing the whole word, saying the letters and paying attention to handwriting joins.
- Sky-write the word.

Snip-snap Head, Ear or Seat?
- Call out words which rhyme with *head*, *ear*, or *seat*.
- Children touch the appropriate part of their body.
- They sit down if they're caught out.
- Keep up a brisk pace.
- Occasionally throw in a catch-you-out (non-rhyming) word to keep everyone alert!

ea and *ear*

NLS objectives for Unit 16
2.3.W1   2.3.W3   2.3.W6   2.3.W11   2.3.W12

Part 2 | You need

Big Book page 33; dry-wipe boards or notebooks; Slips of paper

Whole class
- Write on the board some *ea* words that rhyme with *head* or *seat*, e.g. *bread*, *dead*, *meat*, *treat*.
- Read the introduction on the BBk page.
- Say the words aloud together. Ask: can you hear the two different vowel phonemes? Find words from those written on the board which rhyme with them. Write the rhymes in the correct column of the table.
- Ask children to think of some more words.
- Get Up and Go: children write their words in the right columns.
- Children will come up with words that rhyme but that are not spelt with *ea*. Write these in the catch-you-out box and discuss.
- Remind them of the *ear* sound they investigated in Unit 14. Ask children for words that sound like *ear* and are spelt the same way, e.g. *hear*, *fear* and add to the BBk.
- Write up a short sentence using a word from each column, e.g. *Bread is a treat, my dear!*

Review
- Recap: *ea* can spell different sounds; *ead* is generally 'short' e.
- Discuss catch-you outs, e.g. *read/read*, *lead/lead*, *bead/bread*.
- Homework review.
- What did children find out about *eat*? (it is generally 'long' **ee** phoneme)
- Reinforce the handwriting join for *ea* and ask children to remind you how to join initial and final letters, e.g. *head*, *tea*, *read*.

Follow-up homework
- Children collect from reading books words containing letter pattern *ea* for a class list. They write the words on separate slips of paper, practising handwriting joins. Follow up with Snip-snap *Postbox*.

Test dictation
- OB *After* school we went home quickly.
- A   We sat on a *seat* in the park. Pete had hurt his *head*.
- B   I love to eat brown *bread* with jam. The unkind boy *beat* me.
- C   Jen wore a *neat* new coat.

Snip-snap Postbox
- Make three postboxes out of old cereal packets. Label them *head*, *ear* and *seat*.
- Use words collected from homework or independent activity (written on slips of paper).
- Children take turns to post a word into the correct box.

Snip-snap Full Circle
- Write *play* on the board.
- Tell the children you're going to change one letter at a time to make a new word, until you come full circle back to the word they started with.
- Children write on dry-wipe boards or volunteer to change each word, e.g. *play*, *plan*, *pan*, *man*, *may*, *lay*, and back to *play*.

33

17 Revising vowel phonemes

Objective for Unit 17
To secure phonemic spelling from previous terms

Part 1

You need Big Book page 34; dry-wipe boards or notebooks; Pupil's Book pages 34–35; PCM 17

Whole class
- Tell the children you're going to see if they can remember the different ways of spelling vowel phonemes.
- Look at the BBk page and read the instructions together. (If the children haven't done a wordsearch before, explain that there are words hidden amongst the letters.)
- As the children spot the words, write them under the right headings.
  - 5 **or** sounds: *jaw, morning, small, more, caught*
  - 1 **ar** sound: *farm*
  - 2 **er** sounds: *turn, fur*
  - 1 **oy** sound: *boil*
  - 2 **air** sounds: *chair, rare*
  - 3 **ow** sounds: *how, cow, about*
  - 1 **ai** sound: *sail*
- Time Out...: when the list is complete, brainstorm other words for each sound. Try spelling on dry-wipe boards.
- Show Me: discuss the different ways of spelling the phonemes.
- Introduce the oddbod: *first* – see below.

Pupil activities
A: Search for **ow** and **ar** words (*now, car, arm, about, how, found, park, loud, are*) and sort.
B: Search for **oy** and **air** words (*care, noise, boy, hair, pear, where, toilet, join, air, stare, there, oil*) and add more.
C: Search for **er** and **or** words (*work, cork, short, third, term, word, board, first, her, circle, reward*) and write sentences.

Extra challenge: Search one letter string for **ow, ar, oy, air, er, or**.

Review
- Prepare for homework by demonstrating how to make a word search. Draw a grid as in the BBk and write a word on each row. Fill in with random letters that don't spell anything!
- Recap the six target vowel phonemes **ar/oy/ow/air/or/er**, and some of their common spellings.

Homework Children make up their own wordsearch.

Oddbod first
- Link it with the **ir** sound.
- Make up a phrase or sentence with other ir words, e.g. *my first birthday; girls go first!*
- Write *first* on the board while children sky-write the word.

Snip-snap Phoneme Chain
- Start by writing a 'long' vowel sound on the board, e.g. **oa**.
- The first child says a word using that sound and writes it on the board.
- Carry on round the class until someone drops out.
- Change to a new 'long' vowel sound.

34

Revising vowel phonemes

NLS objectives for Unit 17						
2.1.W3	2.2.W2	2.3.W1	2.3.W4	2.3.W8	2.3.W11	2.3.W12

Part 2 | You need   Big Book page 35; dry-wipe boards or notebooks

Whole class
- Read the limericks on the BBk page together.
- Ask: what do you notice about the rhyming words? (contain 'long' **ee** phonemes and **ee** and **ie** letter patterns)
- Ask them to identify the phonemes **e** and **ee** and associated letter patterns. (**ea**, **ee**, **ie**; Repeat instruction for phoneme **ie** and associated letter patterns **y**, **igh**, **i**.)
- List them on the board and add more words with different letter patterns.
- Have a go at composing a last line for the second limerick (asking children to brainstorm some rhyming words first), e.g. *But never came back from the sky/And left us all wondering why.*

Review
- Recap on the six phonemes **ow**, **ar**, **oy**, **air**, **er**, **or**.
- Introduce some catch-you-outs, e.g. *word/sword*, and ask children to spell them.
- Homework review.
- Volunteers try their wordsearch out on the class (write it on board) and/or children swap their wordsearches with a friend.

Follow-up homework
- Find rhyming pairs with different spellings for **ar**, **oy**, **ow**, **air**, **or**, **er**. Use the pairs later for shared writing.
- Tell the children not to worry about being brilliant poets (it's the process that helps the spellings to stick, not the poetry)!

Test dictation
- OB   His first name is Rob.
- A   Mum found a good photo of me. Ben hurt his arm and his head.
- B   A new boy will join our school on Monday. My bike needs some oil.
- C   The girls were sitting in a circle and singing.

Snip-snap   Which Looks Right?
- Write three alternative spellings on the board, e.g. *nice/nyce/nise*; *flore/floor/flaure*.
- Ask the children to look at the words carefully and decide which is the right spelling.
- Emphasise the useful strategy of trying out different spellings if you're stuck, and asking 'does it look right?'.

Snip-snap   Living Sentences
- Provide a key word cards for each child, making sure there is a mixture of nouns, verbs, adjectives or prepositions.
- Groups of four to six think of a sentence which uses all their words, e.g. *The lazy girl wanted to stay in bed.*
- In turn, groups come to the front, stand in the right order, and say their sentence, holding up cards. Then turn the cards over and all practise spelling.

18 Revision – phonemic spelling, syllables

> **Objectives for Unit 18**
> To revise phonemic spelling; to reinforce work on discriminating syllables

Part 1

You need Big Book page 36; dry-wipe boards or notebooks; Pupil's Book pages 36–37; PCM 18

Whole class
- Explain that in this unit the children are going to find out what a lot they now know.
- Introduce the activity by explaining that sometimes short words are hidden inside longer words. It can help you remember how to spell longer words.
- Demonstrate with the word *become*. Underline *be* and *come*, then underline *me* in a different colour.
- After reading the text on the BBk page, ask children to look at each word very carefully.
- Get Up and Go: invite volunteers to come out and underline hidden words. Start a list on the board. (an, net etc.)
- Time Out: give the children about five minutes to work in pairs, writing the hidden words on dry-wipe boards as they find them.
- Look at *birthday* and *skateboard*. If children have covered Additional Unit 1, can they tell you what these words are called? (compound words, made up of two words stuck together) Look for other compound words. (*everyone, pancakes, ice-cream*)
- Introduce the oddbod: *want* – see below.

Pupil activities
All groups: Look for hidden words using differentiated reading books.

Extra challenge: Children look for the longest hidden word – if they find a five-letter word or longer, they score double.

Review
- Ask children to share their hidden word results.
- Ask: What words are hidden in *hidden*? (hi, I, hid, den)
- Homework review.
- Emphasise useful strategies for learning spellings: look carefully at words; hunt for letter patterns; find words within words; think about the sounds – are there any words that rhyme and are spelt the same way?

Homework
Year 2 oddbod roundup (adapt as appropriate for struggling spellers).

Oddbod want
- To distinguish it from *what*, emphasise that there's no *h*.
- Link it with other *nt* endings: *went*, *sent*.
- Suggest a mnemonic: *I want an ant*.

Snip-snap Word Factory
- Ask children to give you three vowels, then four consonants. Write them on the board.
- Set an egg timer.
- Working in pairs, children make up as many words as they can using the letters on the board.

Revision – phonemic spelling, syllables

NLS objectives for Unit 18					
2.3.W1	2.3.W2	2.3.W4	2.3.W8	2.3.W11	2.3.W12

Part 2   You need   Big Book page 37; dry-wipe boards or notebooks

Whole class
- Check that the children can give examples of a vowel and a consonant.
- Remind them that vowels make different sounds in words, and that some sounds are made up of two vowels put together. Children list all the vowels on dry-wipe boards then say them together. ('short' vowel sounds **a**, **e**, **i**, **o**, **u**).
- Explain that if you say the *names* of the vowels then you get the 'long' vowel phonemes – **ai**, **ee**, **ie**, **oa**, **oo**.
- Ask the children to write words containing each 'long' vowel phoneme on dry-wipe boards.
- Recap common spellings: ai/ay; ee/ea; ie/y/igh; oa/ow; oo/ue/ew.
- Demonstrate handwriting joins as you write up these letter patterns.
- Recap on split digraphs: a-e, i-e, o-e, u-e. (Could play the Snip-snap *Split Digraphs*, see Unit 13, page 27.)
- Look at the BBk page. Explain the meaning of 'all-in-one' – the first sentence contains all the 'long' vowel phonemes listed earlier. (Refer children back to list.) Read the sentence.
- Get Up and Go: children identify each 'long' vowel phoneme.
- Follow the same sequence for split digraphs in the second sentence.
- Compose all-in-one silly sentences, the sillier the better! Brainstorm a list of words before writing.

Review
- Ask the children to tell you some of the things that help them to be good spellers, e.g. looking for hidden words or rhyming words; remembering word families; **Look Say Cover Write Check**; using spelling patterns, etc.
- Homework review.
- Discuss any words that the children still find difficult.

Follow-up homework
- Ask the children to design a Spelling Badge to be awarded when all key words are secure.

Test dictation
- OB   I want to be helpful and cheerful.
- A   Everyone came to my house after school. My birthday is in March.
- B   Jess ate the pancake greedily. Some birds have become very rare.
- C   The noisy girls splashed about in the pool.

Snip-snap   Word Frames
- Write the first and last letters of a word on the board with dashes to represent missing letters, e.g. m_ _t, p_ _l, b_ _t, t_ne.
- Working in pairs on dry-wipe boards, children fill in the gaps to make as many new words as possible.

Snip-snap   Ladder Game
- Draw a ladder on the board.
- Write an initial letter on the first rung, – e.g. s.
- Get Up and Go: children write a two-letter word on the second step, three-letter word on the third step, and so on. Each word must begin with the same initial letter, e.g. *s, so, son, song*.

37

A1 Compound words

Objective for Additional Unit 1
To split familiar compound words into their component parts

Part 1

You need Big Book page 38; dry-wipe boards or notebooks; card strips to build word wall; Pupil's Book pages 38–39; PCM A1

Whole class
- Remind the children of the work on hidden words (Unit 18). Use an example such as *birthday*.
- Explain that lots of long words are made out of two short words put together and they're called *compound* words. If you can spell the short words, it's easy to spell the compound words.
- Ask the children to look on the BBk page for as many pictures of compound words as they can find, e.g. *teapot, teaspoon, teacup, fireman*.
- Write up words on BBk, then write the component words of each compound on card 'bricks' ready for making a wall display later.
- Where appropriate, ask the children to try out spellings on dry-wipe boards.
- Ask: can you think of any other compound words that start with *foot, fire* or *eye*? (e.g. *footprint, footstep; firewood, firework; eyelash, eyelid, eyeball*)
- Write a sentence using suggestions, e.g. *I saw a footprint next to the firewood.*
- Demonstrate handwriting joins.
- Introduce the oddbod: *their* – see below.

Pupil activities
A: Join words to form compounds.
B: As above, then write word definitions.
C: Find compounds that start with given words and write definitions.

Extra challenge: Think of compound words that end in *man*.

Review
- Recap on the definition of *compound word*.
- Ask volunteers from group C to share their compound words.
- Make more card 'brick' pairs for the word wall.

Homework Children look for compound words to add to the wall display.

Oddbod their
- Emphasise that it isn't *ie*.
- Look at beginning: see the hidden word *the*.
- Say '*the plus ir*' as you write the letters on the board.
- Children do the same on dry-wipe boards.
- Learn it with other personal pronouns: *my, his, our*.
- Use it in sentences.

Snip-snap Word Wall
- Use the compound word wall for a range of sorting activities, e.g. children race to write down as many compound words as they can on a given theme.
- You could have words: connected with parts of the body; containing a particular letter; containing a particular vowel phoneme; with a given consonant cluster; with a given number of letters, etc.

38

Compound words

NLS objectives for Additional Unit 1
2.2.W4   2.2.W6   2.2.W9   2.2.W14

Part 2

You need Big Book page 39; dry-wipe boards or notebooks; enough word cards for everyone in the class (use words which will make compound words from BBk and pupil activities, etc.)

Whole class
- Read the BBk page together.
- Point out how to start with the second word in working out the meaning.
- Ask volunteers to complete the definitions.
- Give out word cards (compound pairs) to groups of four to six, with a card for each child. Children find their partner to make a compound word.
- Each pair works out the meaning of their word.
- Compose compound word sentences together, e.g. *The snowman sat by the fireplace all weekend*.

Review
- Pairs take it in turns to display their compound word and explain its meaning.
- Homework review.
- Make new cards from homework words to add to the word wall. Demonstrate handwriting joins as you write the words.

Follow-up homework
- Children make up sentences using personal pronouns (see oddbod).

Test dictation
- OB Dan and Sue found the dog and got their reward.
- A   A lot of girls are good at football. My dad works on the railway.
- B   It is a treat to see a rainbow. After school we do our homework.
- C   At the weekend people try not to go to work.

Snip-snap Compound Clues
- Give children a clue for a compound word, e.g. *the place you sleep in*: bedroom.
- Children guess the word.
- Children identify the two separate words.
- Working in pairs, children write the compound word on dry-wipe boards.
- Add the words to the word wall.

Snip-snap Shannon's Game
(Like Hangman, but you have to guess the letters in order. A useful assessment activity, revealing children's understanding of letter order, likely combinations, etc. Use BBk page 44.)
- Choose a key word.
- Write the first letter on the board.
- Children guess the next letter.
- Write correct letters in order, keeping a checklist of incorrect letters guessed.

39

A2 Revision of prefixes and suffixes; puzzle letter

Objectives for Additional Unit 2
To spell words with common prefixes to indicate the negative; to spell words with common suffixes; to spell key words

Part 1

You need Big Book page 40; dry-wipe boards or notebooks; Pupil's Book pages 40–41; PCM A2

Whole class
- Ask the children to define *prefix* and *suffix*
- Recap: it's easy adding prefixes – you just add them! However, there are some catch-you-outs to look out for when you add a suffix, e.g. dropping the last *e*; *y* changes to *i*; doubling the consonant if it ends in a single vowel and a consonant. (Don't labour these – they will be dealt with in more detail in Year 3.)
- Read the words and parts of words on the BBk page. Identify which are prefixes, suffixes and root words.
- Ask: can anybody find a bit to join up with the whole word *wind* to make a new word?
- Do one example together on the board, e.g. *unwind*.
- Children experiment on dry-wipe boards to make other words, e.g. *rewind*, *windless*.
- Discuss the two pronunciations and meanings of *wind/wind*.
- Experiment with another root word, e.g. *do*.
- Introduce the oddbod: *eight* – see below.

Pupil activities
A: Add ed or ly to given words to make new words and write sentences.
B: Adding prefix or suffix to given words to make new words.
C: As B.

Think about...: Think of words beginning with mis.

Review
- Make a list of the words the children have made.
- Recap on the meanings of *prefix* and *suffix*.

Homework Children look in their reading books for words with suffixes and investigate most and the least common suffixes found.

Oddbod eight
- This oddbod is really odd! It sounds like *ate* but couldn't be more different!
- Identify the 'long' phoneme **ai** spelt **eigh**, as in *neigh*, *sleigh*. Add this spelling to the other ways of spelling 'long' **a** (**ae**/**ai** phoneme).
- Write it on the board, demonstrating handwriting joins.
- Sky-write the word.

Snip-snap Quick Change
- Write a regular verb on the board, e.g. *jump*.
- Call out the word with a suffix added, e.g. *jumping/jumps/jumped*.
- Children write the new word as quickly as they can.
- The first to finish can say the next verb.
- Alternatively, pairs of children come up with new words as quickly as possible (adding suffixes to given verb). The aim is to make as many new words as possible.

Revision of prefixes and suffixes; puzzle letter

NLS objectives for Additional Unit 2
2.2.W8   2.3.W7   2.3.W8   2.3.W11   2.3.W12

Part 2   **You need**   Big Book page 41; dry-wipe boards or notebooks

Whole class
- Let the children have a moment or two to look at the puzzle letter on the BBk page. Ask them if they can guess what the first line says. Explain that the puzzle uses pictures as well as letters.
- Start to decode it together, showing them how one letter is crossed out and another one put in its place, e.g. *pen/Jen*.
- Write the finished letter on the board, asking children to contribute some of the words.

Dear Jen
How are you? I hope you get well again soon. I had a good time at our Dad's house. What do you want for tea when you come home? Ring and tell me.
Love from
Mike

- Compose a reply from Jen to Mike – either a puzzle or straightforward letter, using some key words.

Review
- Look at *ear* and brainstorm other words which rhyme but are spelt differently, e.g. *here*, *cheer*.
- Look at *house* and change the first letter to make another word, e.g. *mouse, louse*.
- Homework review.
- Discuss the results of the suffix hunt. Which words did children find? Which seem to be the most and least common suffixes?

Test dictation
OB   Soon I will be *eight*.
A   The dustbin smelled *strongly* of fish. The cow *jumped* over the moon.
B   A lot of big dogs are *harmless*. Mum helped me to *untie* my football boots.
C   What are you *doing* at the weekend?

Snip-snap   Key Word Tennis
- Say a high frequency word. Pairs write it on dry-wipe boards.
- Choose a pair to write the word on the board.
- Use tennis scoring: children get a point for every word correctly spelt; you get the point if it's wrong!

Snip-snap   Clusters Competition
- Write initial consonant clusters on the board, e.g. *st*, *br*, *pl*, *th*.
- Start an egg timer.
- Before the timer runs out, children write on dry-wipe boards as many words as possible that start with those letters.

41

A3 Synonyms

Objective for Additional Unit 3
To collect and use synonyms, discussing shades of meaning

Part 1

You need Big Book page 42; dry-wipe boards or notebooks; Pupil's Book pages 42–43; PCM A3

Whole class
- Ask the children to imagine a giant and tell you what they can see in their mind's eye. Look at the BBk page: does their giant look like this?
- Read the words around the giant: *big, large, huge, enormous*. Why do they think the words are getting bigger? (*Enormous* is bigger than *big*)
- Brainstorm other words meaning 'big', e.g. *great, grand, immense, colossal, gigantic*. Discuss shades of meaning – which do they think is the biggest of all?
- Time Out/Show Me: children try spelling the words on dry-wipe boards. Discuss results.
- Look at the small beetle on the BBk page and discuss *tiny* in a similar way.
- Brainstorm other words meaning 'small'. Discuss shades of meaning.
- Write *cross* on the board. Brainstorm other words meaning the same, e.g. *angry, furious*. Discuss gradations of meaning.
- Explain that they have been making *synonyms*. Synonym means a word that has the same or nearly the same meaning as another word.

Pupil activities
A: Match synonym pairs and practise spelling.
B: Find synonyms for given words and think of others.
C: Think of synonyms for *cold* and use them in a short description.

Extra challenge: Think of synonyms for *hot*.

Review
- Recap: when a word means the same (or nearly the same) as another word, it is called a *synonym*. Explain that when a word means the opposite of another word it is called an *antonym*. Briefly recap on opposites from Unit 12.

Homework Children make words out of *enormous* and *gigantic*.

Oddbod many
- Identify the tricky bit – a sounds like 'short' **e**.
- Link it with *any*.
- Work out a mnemonic, e.g. **m**ost **a**nts **n**ever **y**awn.

Snip-snap Synonym Pelmanism
- Make up synonym pairs of varying difficulty, e.g. *big/huge, small/tiny, happy/joyful, afraid/scared, dirty/mucky*. Write each word on a separate post-it.
- Stick the words on the board in random order. Ask children to come up and put pairs together.

Synonyms

> **NLS objectives for Additional Unit 3**
> 2.2.W11   2.3.W10   2.3.W12

Part 2 | You need
Big Book page 43; small sticky labels

Whole class
- Read the nursery rhymes in the BBk aloud together. Then read the instructions.
- Focus on the words in blue. Brainstorm possible synonyms for each blue word in turn, e.g. *little*: *small*, *tiny*. (Ask children what they think a *tuffet* is – probably a hillock or mound.)
- Agree on one synonym for each word focusing on why some words are better choices because they are closer to the original meaning, e.g. *small* is a better synonym than *tiny* in this case. Write the word on a sticky label, demonstrating handwriting joins.
- Cover the word in the BBk with the sticky label. Read the new version through together.
- Write up another rhyme, e.g. *Old King Cole*, and replace words with synonyms.

Review
- Reinforce terms *synonym* and *antonym* by looking at examples of both.
- Homework review.
- Discuss the words and check spellings.

Follow-up homework
- Change some words in another nursery rhyme, using either synonyms or antonyms.

Test dictation
- OB   Many rare birds live in the park.
- A   The big bathroom was very cold. The little boys ran about the playground.
- B   I took a photo of the small church. I had a large ice-cream for a treat.
- C   My dad gets angry if I misbehave.

Snip-snap   Antonyms
- Use the BBk nursery rhymes.
- Find opposites for the blue words.
- Spell them on dry-wipe boards first, then write labels.
- Read the new version.
- Reinforce the term *antonym*.

Snip-snap   Word Hunt
- Write a fairly long word on the board, e.g. *because*.
- Show the children how to jumble the letters up. Write the letters in a different order.
- Find other words, e.g. *be*, *cause*, *use*, *case*, *base*, *cube*.
- Try the same game using the name of your school.

43

Facsimile Big Book pages

This section contains facsimiles of the Big Book pages for ease of planning.

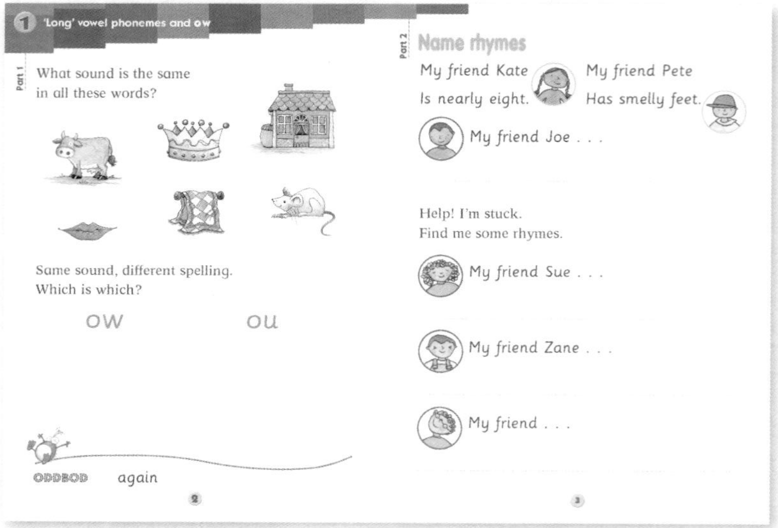

1 'Long' vowel phonemes and ow
Part 1

What sound is the same in all these words?

Same sound, different spelling. Which is which?

ow
ou

ODD BOD again

Name rhymes
Part 2

My friend Kate Is nearly eight.
My friend Pete Has smelly feet.

My friend Joe . . .

Help! I'm stuck. Find me some rhymes.

My friend Sue . . . .

My friend Zane . . . .

My friend . . . .

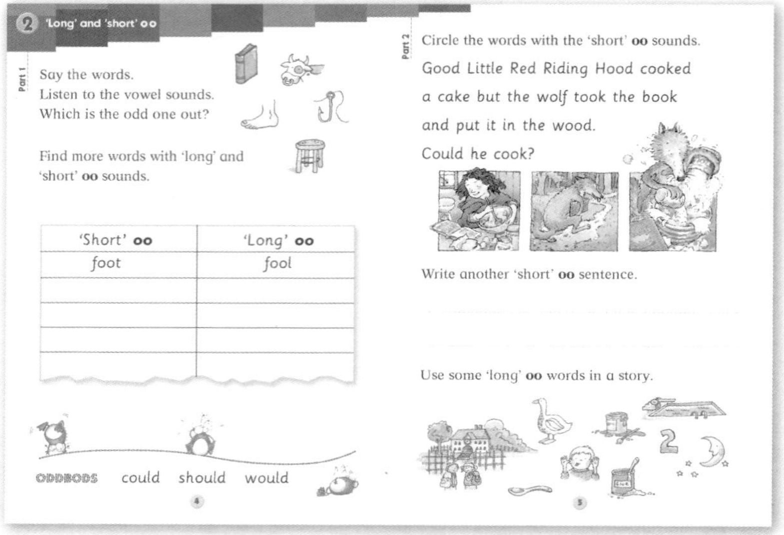

2 'Long' and 'short' oo
Part 1

Say the words. Listen to the vowel sounds. Which is the odd one out?

Find more words with 'long' and 'short' **oo** sounds.

'Short' **oo**	'Long' **oo**
foot	fool

ODD BOD   could   should   would

Part 2

Circle the words with the 'short' **oo** sounds.

Good Little Red Riding Hood cooked a cake but the wolf took the book and put it in the wood. Could he cook?

Write another 'short' **oo** sentence.

Use some 'long' **oo** words in a story.

3 Plurals
Part 1

Add s to each animal name.

Noah's ark

The animals went in two by two;
The elephant went with the kangaroo
The animals went in four by four;
The pig and the goat got stuck in the door.
The animals went in six by six;
The cow and the horse were up to tricks.

ODD BOD   to   too   two

Old Macdonald's farm
Part 2

Finish the spelling sums.

Old Macdonald had a farm,
Ee-i ee-i o!
And on that farm he had some   (cow + s = ?)
And on that farm he had some   (pig + s = ?)
And on that farm he had some   (goat + s = ?)
And on that farm he had some   (chick + s = ?)

HAVE A GO

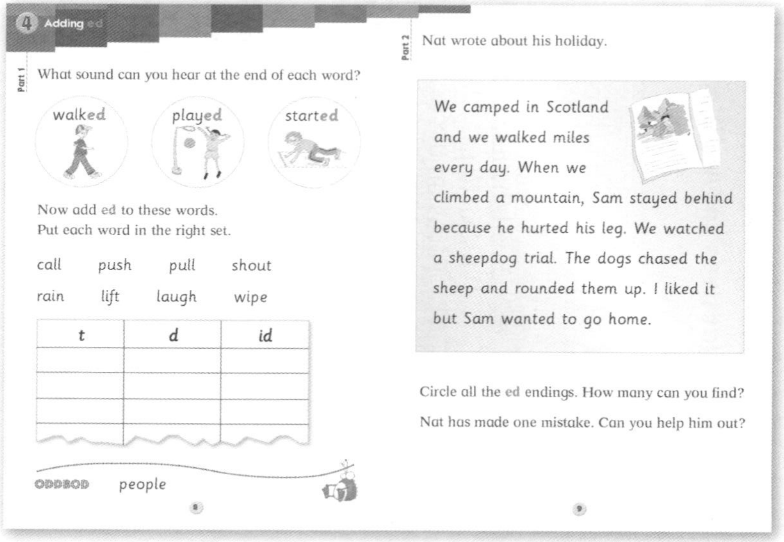

4 Adding ed
Part 1

What sound can you hear at the end of each word?

walked   played   started

Now add ed to these words.
Put each word in the right set.

call   push   pull   shout
rain   lift   laugh   wipe

t	d	id

ODD BOD   people

Part 2

Nat wrote about his holiday.

We camped in Scotland and we walked miles every day. When we climbed a mountain, Sam stayed behind because he hurted his leg. We watched a sheepdog trial. The dogs chased the sheep and rounded them up. I liked it but Sam wanted to go home.

Circle all the ed endings. How many can you find?
Nat has made one mistake. Can you help him out?

44

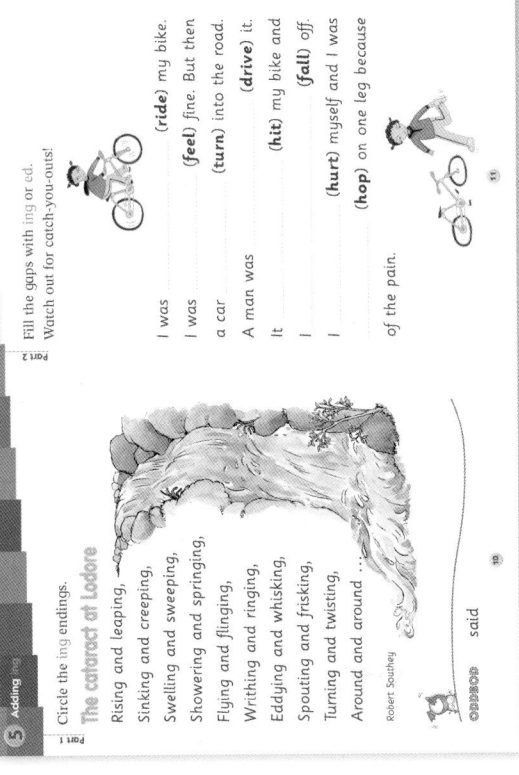

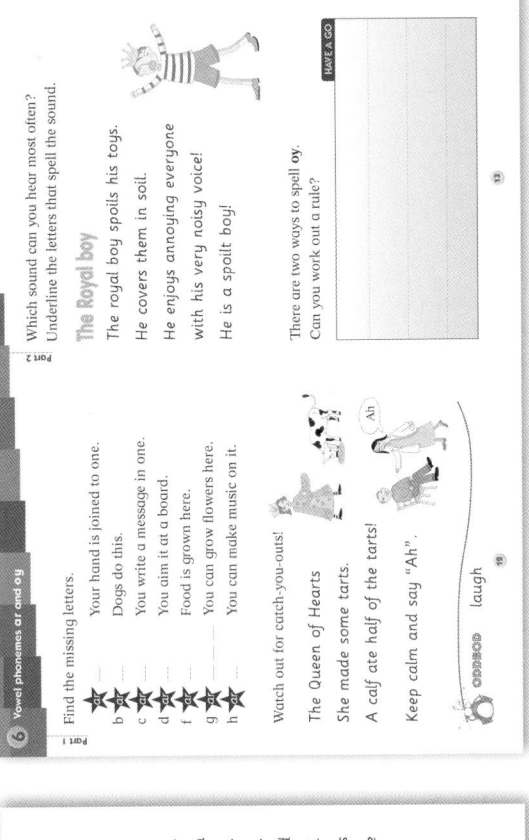

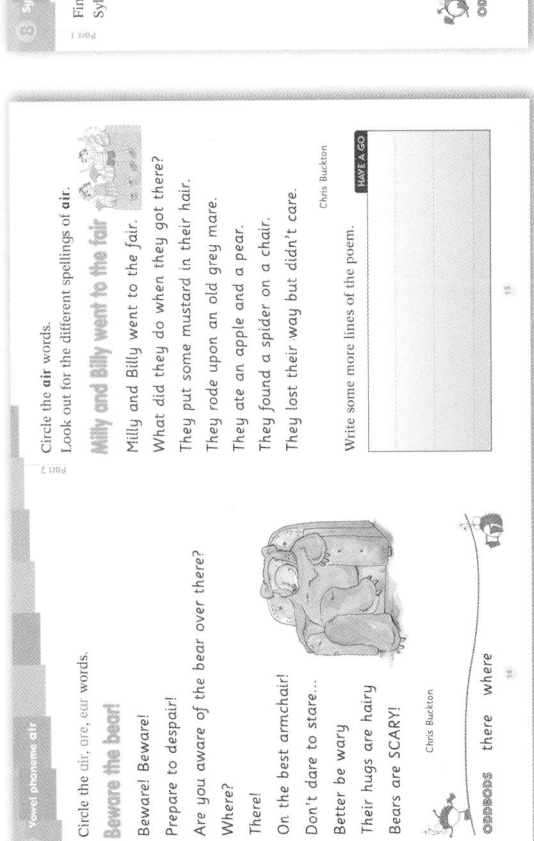

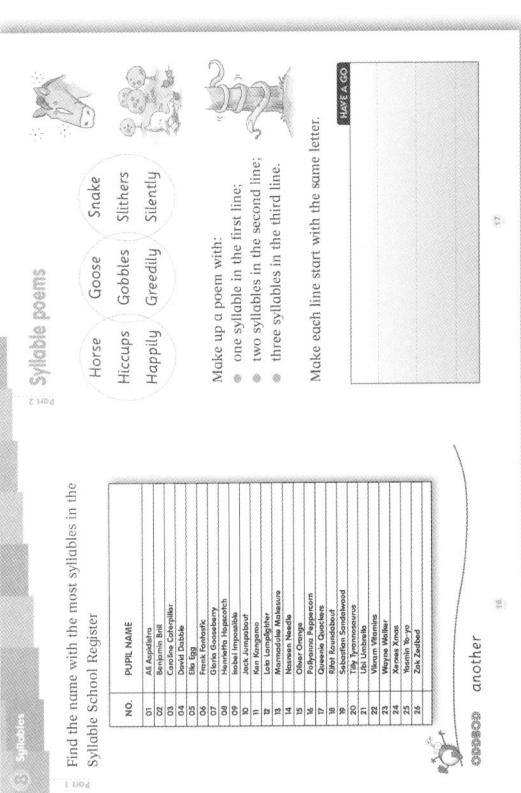

Facsimile Big Book pages cont.

5 Adding ing

Part 1

Circle the ing endings.

The cataract at Lodore

Rising and leaping,
Sinking and creeping,
Swelling and sweeping,
Showering and springing,
Flying and flinging,
Writhing and ringing,
Eddying and whisking,
Spouting and frisking,
Turning and twisting,
Around and around …

Robert Southey

said

Part 2

Fill the gaps with ing or ed.
Watch out for catch-you-outs!

I was _____ (ride) my bike.
I was _____ (feel) fine. But then
a car _____ (turn) into the road.
A man was _____ (drive) it.
It _____ (hit) my bike and
I _____ (fall) off.
I _____ (hurt) myself and I was
_____ (hop) on one leg because
of the pain.

6 Vowel phonemes or and oy

Part 1

Find the missing letters.

b ★ _____ Your hand is joined to one.
c ★ _____ Dogs do this.
d ★ _____ You write a message in one.
e ★ _____ You aim it at a board.
f ★ _____ Food is grown here.
g ★ _____ You can grow flowers here.
h ★ _____ You can make music on it.

Watch out for catch-you-outs!

The Queen of Hearts
She made some tarts.
A calf ate half of the tarts!
Keep calm and say "Ah".

laugh

Part 2

Which sound can you hear most often?
Underline the letters that spell the sound.

The Royal boy

The royal boy spoils his toys.
He covers them in soil.
He enjoys annoying everyone
with his very noisy voice!
He is a spoilt boy!

There are two ways to spell **oy**.
Can you work out a rule?

HAVE A GO

7 Vowel phonemes air

Part 1

Circle the air, are, ear words.

Beware the bear!

Beware! Beware!
Prepare to despair!
Are you aware of the bear over there?
Where?
There!
On the best armchair!
Don't dare to stare…
Better be wary
Their hugs are hairy
Bears are SCARY!

Chris Buckton

there   where

Part 2

Circle the **air** words.
Look out for the different spellings of **air**.

Milly and Billy went to the fair

Milly and Billy went to the fair.
What did they do when they got there?
They put some mustard in their hair.
They rode upon an old grey mare.
They ate an apple and a pear.
They found a spider on a chair.
They lost their way but didn't care.

Chris Buckton

Write some more lines of the poem.

HAVE A GO

8 Syllables

Part 1

Find the name with the most syllables in the Syllable School Register

01	PUPIL NAME
01	Ali Aspidistra
02	Benjamin Brill
03	Caroline Caterpillar
04	David Dabble
05	Elle Egg
06	Frank Fantastic
07	Gloria Gooseberry
08	Henrietta Hopscotch
09	Isobel Impossible
10	Jack Jumpalot
11	Ken Kangaroo
12	Lola Lamplighter
13	Marmaduke Molossus
14	Naureen Needle
15	Oliver Orange
16	Pollyanna Peppercorn
17	Queenie Quackers
18	Rifat Roundabout
19	Sebastian Sandalwood
20	Tilly Tyrannosaurus
21	Ubi Umbrella
22	Viccum Vitamins
23	Wayne Walker
24	Xerxes Xmas
25	Yasmin Yo-yo
26	Zak Zedbed

another

Part 2

Syllable poems

Horse   Goose   Snake
Hiccups   Gobbles   Slithers
Happily   Greedily   Silently

Make up a poem with:
- one syllable in the first line;
- two syllables in the second line;
- three syllables in the third line.

Make each line start with the same letter.

HAVE A GO

Facsimile Big Book pages cont.

9 Vowel phoneme er

Part 1

What sound is the same in all these words?

bird   fur   girl   turn   first
circle   turkey   kerb   church
whirl   skirt   birth   burger
fern   term   dirty   purr   burn

Sort them into three groups.

bird	fur	term

ODD BOD   were

Part 2

What are the names for people who:

bike? _____   swim? _____
bake? _____   sing? _____

Watch out for the catch-you-outs!

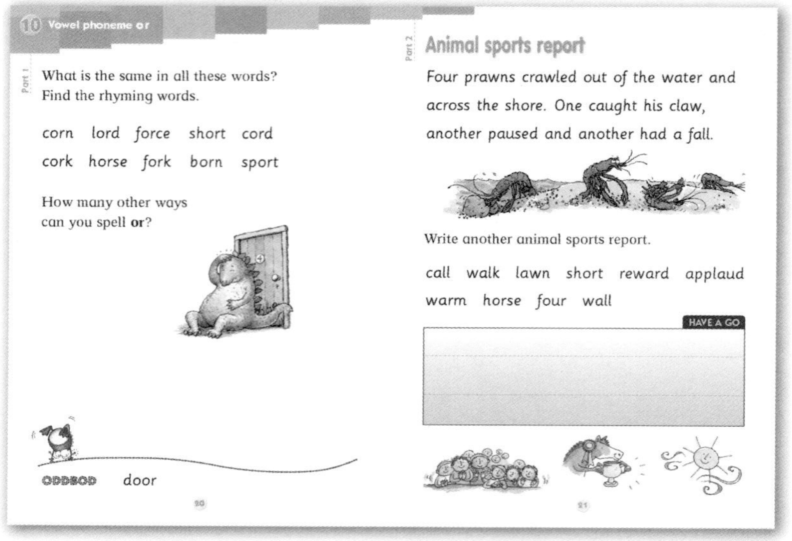

10 Vowel phoneme o.r

Part 1

What is the same in all these words?
Find the rhyming words.

corn   lord   force   short   cord
cork   horse   fork   born   sport

How many other ways can you spell **or**?

ODD BOD   door

Part 2 — Animal sports report

Four prawns crawled out of the water and across the shore. One caught his claw, another paused and another had a fall.

Write another animal sports report.

call   walk   lawn   short   reward   applaud
warm   horse   four   wall

HAVE A GO

---

11 Digraphs -n ch and f phoneme

Part 1

Look for two consonants making one sound.

Where?   What?   Which?   Why?

ODD BOD   who

Part 2

What sound is the same in all these words?

safe   fire
telephone   chief
graph   elephant   tough
laugh   cliff

f	gh	ph	ff

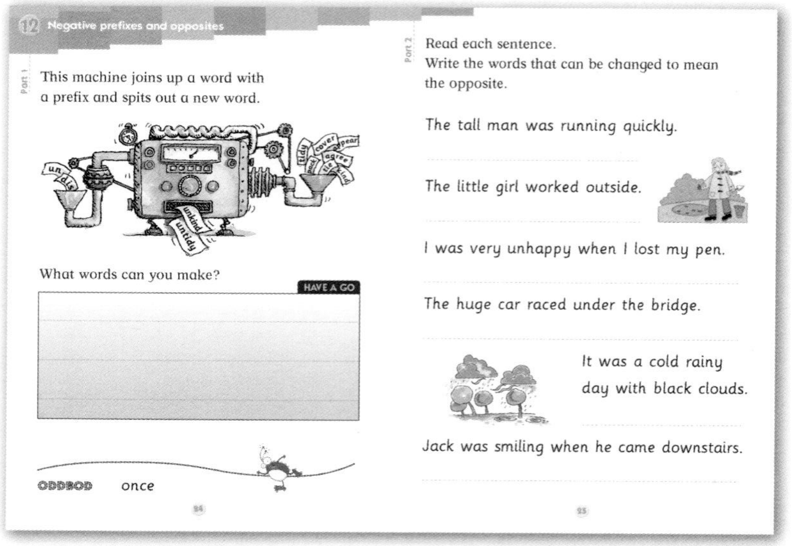

12 Negative prefixes and opposites

Part 1

This machine joins up a word with a prefix and spits out a new word.

What words can you make?

HAVE A GO

ODD BOD   once

Part 3

Read each sentence.
Write the words that can be changed to mean the opposite.

The tall man was running quickly.

The little girl worked outside.

I was very unhappy when I lost my pen.

The huge car raced under the bridge.

It was a cold rainy day with black clouds.

Jack was smiling when he came downstairs.

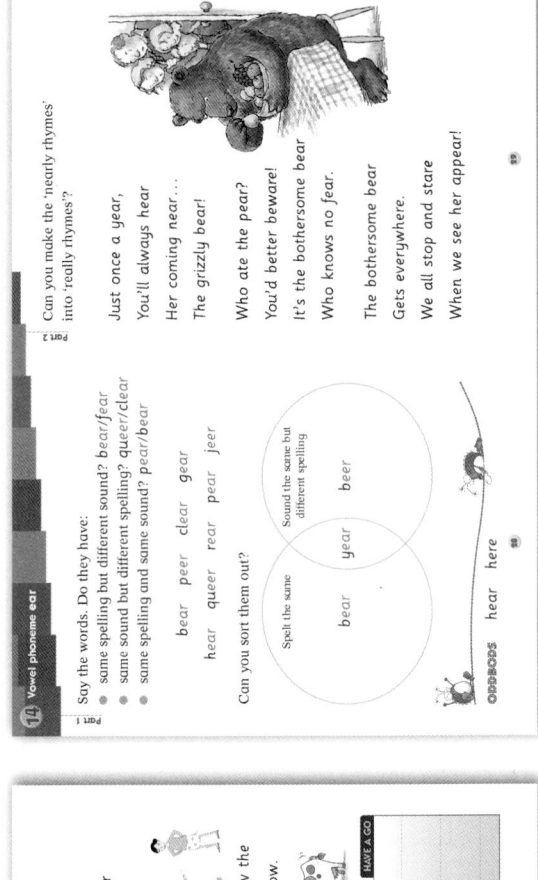

Facsimile Big Book pages cont.

13 Some spelling pattern, different sounds

Part 1

Find the odd one out in each sentence.

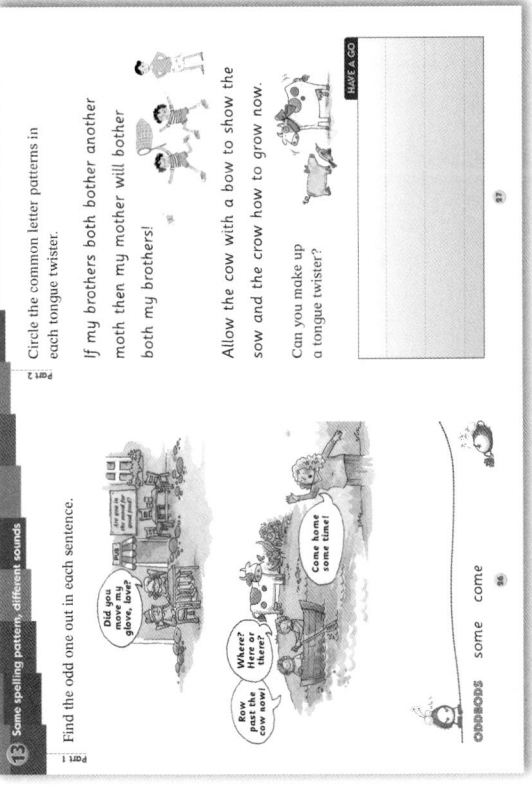

Part 2

Circle the common letter patterns in each tongue twister.

If my brothers both bother another moth then my mother will bother both my brothers!

Allow the cow with a bow to show the sow and the crow how to grow now.

Can you make up a tongue twister?

HAVE A GO

ODDBODS   some   come

14 Vowel phoneme ear

Part 1

Say the words. Do they have:
- same spelling but different sound? bear/fear
- same sound but different spelling? queer/clear
- same spelling and same sound? pear/bear

bear   peer   clear   gear
hear   queer   rear   pear   jeer

Can you sort them out?

Spelt the same	Sound the same but different spelling
bear	beer
year	

Part 2

Can you make the 'nearly rhymes' into 'really rhymes'?

Just once a year,
You'll always hear
Her coming near....
The grizzly bear!

Who ate the pear?
You'd better beware!
It's the bothersome bear
Who knows no fear.

The bothersome bear
Gets everywhere.
We all stop and stare
When we see her appear!

ODDBODS   hear   here

15 Adding suffix

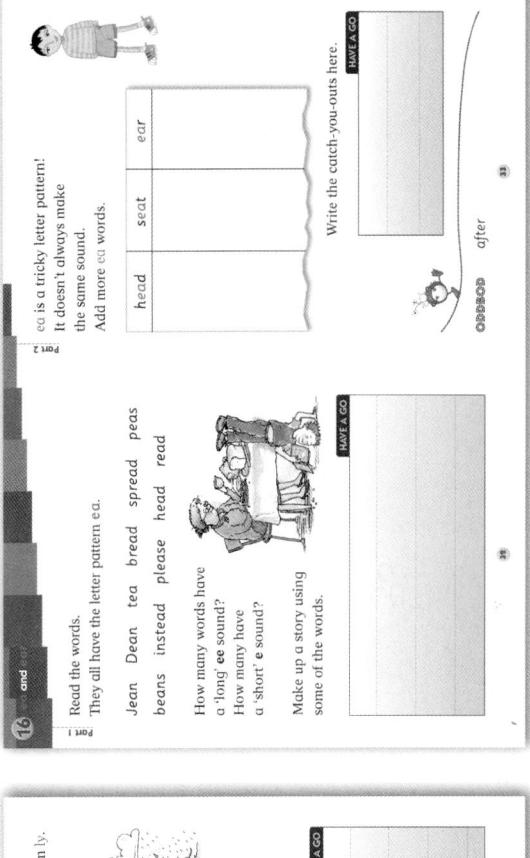

Part 1

Match each word to the right picture.

quick   sad   happy   lazy
slow   cross   lucky   sleepy

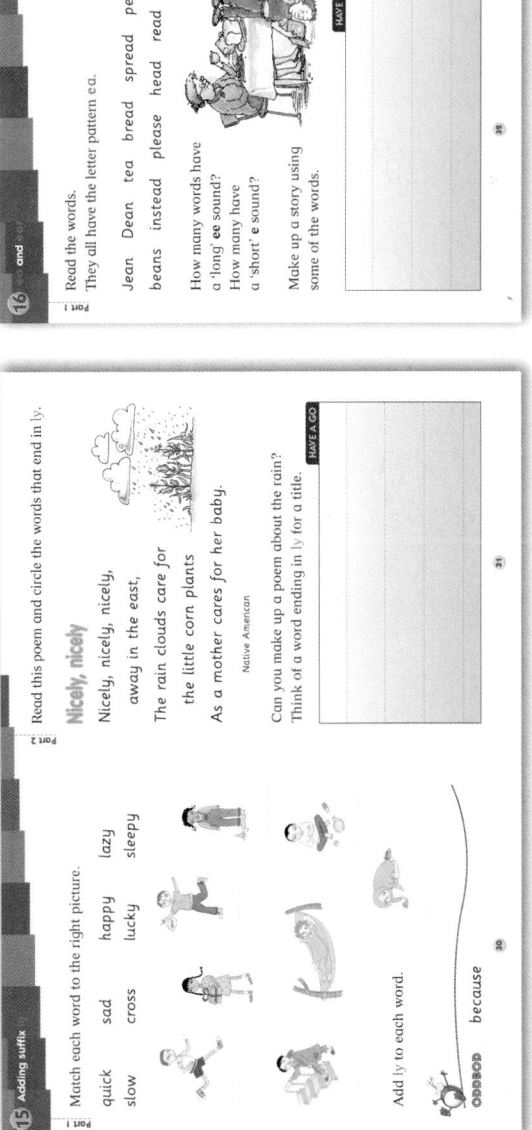

Add *ly* to each word.

ODDBODS   because

Part 2

Read this poem and circle the words that end in *ly*.

Nicely, nicely

Nicely, nicely, nicely,
away in the east,
The rain clouds care for
the little corn plants
As a mother cares for her baby.

Native American

Can you make up a poem about the rain? Think of a word ending in *ly* for a title.

HAVE A GO

16 ea and ee

Part 1

Read the words.
They all have the letter pattern ea.

Jean   Dean   tea   bread   spread   peas
beans   instead   please   head   read

How many words have a 'long' **ee** sound?
How many have a 'short' **e** sound?

Make up a story using some of the words.

HAVE A GO

Part 2

ea is a tricky letter pattern!
It doesn't always make the same sound.
Add more *ea* words.

head	seat	ear

Write the catch-you-outs here.

HAVE A GO

ODDBODS   after

47

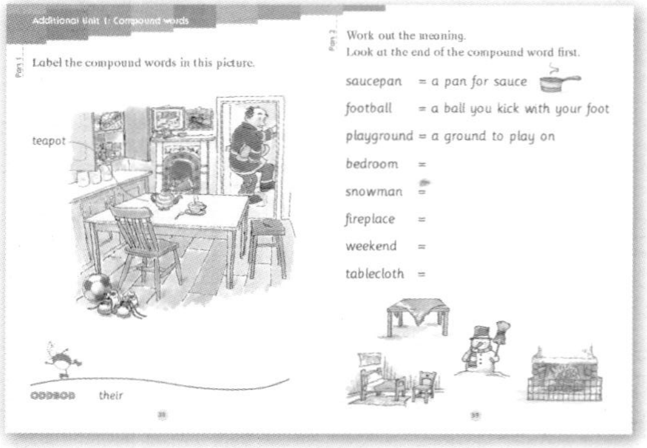

Facsimile Big Book pages cont.

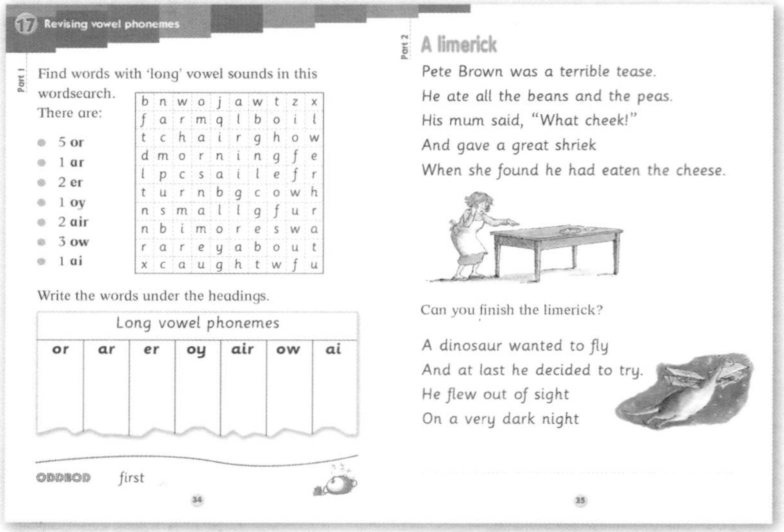

17 Revising vowel phonemes

Part 1

Find words with 'long' vowel sounds in this wordsearch.
There are:
- 5 **or**
- 1 **ar**
- 2 **er**
- 1 **oy**
- 2 **air**
- 3 **ow**
- 1 **ai**

b	n	w	o	j	a	w	t	z	x
f	a	r	m	q	l	b	o	i	l
t	c	h	a	i	r	g	h	o	w
d	m	o	r	n	i	n	g	f	e
l	p	c	s	a	i	l	e	f	r
t	u	r	n	b	g	c	o	w	h
n	s	m	a	l	l	g	f	u	r
n	b	i	m	o	r	e	s	w	a
r	a	r	e	y	a	b	o	u	t
x	c	a	u	g	h	t	w	f	u

Write the words under the headings.

	Long vowel phonemes					
or	**ar**	**er**	**oy**	**air**	**ow**	**ai**

first

A limerick

Part 2

Pete Brown was a terrible tease.
He ate all the beans and the peas.
His mum said, "What cheek!"
And gave a great shriek
When she found he had eaten the cheese.

Can you finish the limerick?

A dinosaur wanted to fly
And at last he decided to try.
He flew out of sight
On a very dark night
_____

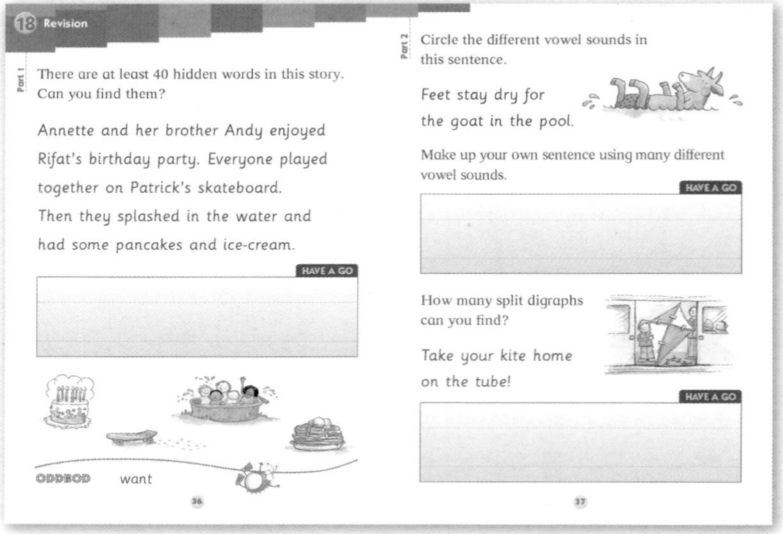

18 Revision

Part 1

There are at least 40 hidden words in this story.
Can you find them?

Annette and her brother Andy enjoyed Rifat's birthday party. Everyone played together on Patrick's skateboard. Then they splashed in the water and had some pancakes and ice-cream.

HAVE A GO
_____

want

Part 2

Circle the different vowel sounds in this sentence.

Feet stay dry for
the goat in the pool.

Make up your own sentence using many different vowel sounds.

HAVE A GO
_____

How many split digraphs can you find?

Take your kite home
on the tube!

ACEnglish Unit 1: Compound words

Part 1

Label the compound words in this picture.

teapot   their

Work out the meaning.
Look at the end of the compound word first.
- saucepan = a pan for sauce
- football = a ball you kick with your foot
- playground = a ground to play on
- bedroom =
- snowman =
- fireplace =
- weekend =
- tablecloth =

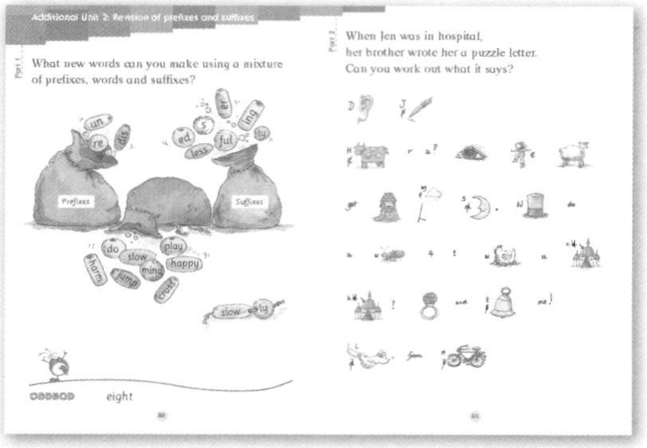

ACEnglish Unit 2: Revision of prefixes and suffixes

Part 1

What new words can you make using a mixture of prefixes, words and suffixes?

eight

Part 2

When Jen was in hospital, her brother wrote her a puzzle letter. Can you work out what it says?

ACEnglish Unit 3: Synonyms

Part 1

Enormous

Write other words that mean 'big' or 'huge'.

many

Part 2

Change the blue words in these nursery rhymes to words which mean nearly the same.

Little Jack Horner
Sat in the corner,
Eating his Christmas pie.
He put in his thumb
And pulled out a plum
And said "What a good boy am I!"

Little Miss Muffet
Sat on a tuffet,
Eating her curds and whey.
There came a big spider,
That sat down beside her
And frightened Miss Muffet away.

48